DEAF TIPS

POWERFUL COMMUNICATION

Twelve lessons from the Deaf world to improve communication in
your personal, social, and professional life

Bruno Paul Kahne, PhD

Illustrations by Stéphane Janda
www.bienvustudio.com

To Noam, Tom, and Liam:
May you always be
Men of love
Men of justice
Men of communication

Contents

Preface

When you appreciate something about someone, do you tell that person? Are you able to defend your point of view without becoming aggressive? Do you *really* listen to others when their views are different from yours? Are you able to say no to people you love or are afraid of? Do you understand when people say no even if they don't use the word? When you don't understand something, do you admit it? Do you let other people finish their sentences? Do you listen more than you talk? Do you see when the body language of people doesn't correspond to what they are saying? When someone has hurt your feelings, do you express your emotions to that person? Are you aware of the emotions you trigger in the people who are listening to you? Do you remain focused when the person who is talking is not concise? Are you comfortable when someone pays you a compliment?

If your honest answer to most of these questions is *no*, then this book, *Deaf Tips*, is definitely for you.

Books on communication have always been written by Hearing people for Hearing people. But who are those writers to position themselves as teachers? What credentials do they have to give lessons to others? Who can believe that they always actively listen to their spouses, patiently talk with their children, empathize with their suppliers, reformulate and check understanding with their clients, and never criticize their managers? Don't they struggle, as we all do, in their daily communication with others… and with themselves? And if they are not the best teachers, who are? To find them, we must follow Canadian philosopher Marshall McLuhan's prescription: a fish cannot discover water.

Often considered as deficient in communication because they can't hear, and frequently can't talk, Deaf people have been rejected from the aquarium for the last centuries. The reality is, however, that they are better communicators, passing messages much faster and more precisely than any Hearing person. In this book Deaf people share all the tips and tricks they use to be effective communicators.

As the world moves away from discrimination and narrow-mindedness, it is time to recognize the real experts in communication and learn from them.

Background

In November 2006, a trainee came to see me at the end of a communication course and handed me a piece of paper with the name of a man and his phone number written on it, and asked me to call that person. I asked him why. He replied, in a puzzling way, that he didn't know, but was convinced that I wouldn't regret it. I was somewhat taken aback but the mystery aroused my curiosity and I called the person the following day. I introduced myself and asked if we could meet. On the other end of the receiver a man asked me why we should meet, and I told him, slightly embarrassed, that I didn't know, but that we had a friend in common who thought it would be a good idea. A few days later I met François who told me his story:

François: I started my career as an Airbus engineer, but quickly became interested by the intercultural aspects of the company. My English was good, so I was often asked to facilitate heated debates between German, French, Spanish, and British managers.

Bruno: Did you like it?

François: Very much. I was in my early thirties and, compared to others, I was clearly on a fast track. Then, we had our third baby. A big, smiling, baby boy with huge blue eyes. Everything was perfect; it was the best of all possible worlds. But after a few months we felt that something was wrong. He was always looking at his hands, or looking at sources of light, and he didn't sleep well at night. So, we went to see a doctor.

Bruno: What did the doctor say?

François: He confirmed that there was a problem and sent us to a hospital for more tests. After the tests, the doctor called us into his office, and told us that our son might be autistic, that she wasn't sure yet, but that we should prepare ourselves for it. My wife rejected the diagnosis outright. She didn't even want to hear the word *autistic*.

Bruno: How old was your son at the time?

François: He was 2 ½ years old and he still couldn't speak. So the doctors taught us how to deal with autism. The psychologists, for example, had asked us to ignore him when he was trying to get attention by pulling our clothes in order to force him to speak. We followed their recommendations, since after all, they were the experts. It took us some time to understand that by doing so, our son really was becoming autistic.

Bruno: Becoming? What do you mean? He wasn't autistic?

François: Well, I had accepted his autism, but my wife kept on insisting that he was not. She thought he had a hearing problem. The psychologist got fed up with her insistence and sent us to a hospital for a series of tests with the boy put to sleep to have objective results. They took me aside and told me that once the tests were over, my wife would have to face the truth, and consequently might become depressed. I took the day off and went to the hospital to give her some moral support.

Bruno: And what happened?

François: At the end of the day, as we were waiting for our son to wake up, a nurse came into the room. We asked her for the results. She looked embarrassed and asked us to wait for the doctor. We insisted and she finally told us that, indeed, our son was not autistic. He was completely deaf.

Bruno: Deaf? How did you react?

François: We were so happy! Our son was *only* deaf! I went back to see the psychologist to tell her the good news. Her response was that our son might not be just deaf, but might have additional problems as well! I was shocked. How could she say that to justify her wrong diagnosis? From that day on, we decided to only trust our instincts. I explained to my manager: that I needed to learn how to communicate with my son. With the support of the HR dept. he found a way to finance three months of complete immersion in Sign Language for my wife and me. At the end of the first day we came back home and communicated with our son for the first time.

Bruno: What do you mean "for the first time"?

François: Well, we saw on that first day how Deaf people behave together, and we simply did the same with our son, for example, placing one hand on his shoulder to call him. For the first time, he looked us straight in the eyes. Something he had given up doing with us a long time ago. Then, we started to sign *sleep* before going to bed, *eat* when cooking, etc. A few days later, Thomas stood in front of me, and made the sign *eat*. He was hungry, and he was expressing it! I started to cry. I gave him food, and he smiled. He was three years old. From then on his behavior completely changed.

Bruno: And what happened at the end of the three months of immersion?

François: I returned to Airbus with a new competence. I could speak Sign Language in an environment where everybody else spoke a different spoken language.

Bruno: Why do you say it was a new competence? Nobody speaks Sign Language in Airbus.

François: I know. But now I could see things that I had never seen before. I was not just listening to the words people were saying, I was also reading their body language. This helped me to get back on the fast track again, working during the day on aerospace projects, and at night for a Deaf association. Step by step, my involvement in the association took over. With the support of my manager, I presented Airbus the project of using new communication technologies to help the Deaf world. Airbus liked the idea and decided to sponsor me. I told my family that nothing would change, but of course everything did.

The story moved me beyond expectation. I kept thinking about it over and over. Francois' eyes were full of light, his voice full of faith, and his words full of conviction. His whole body radiated energy. It was a very special meeting, but I had no idea of what to do next. A week later, however, a client told me with much sarcasm that a course on communication I had developed was not challenging enough. At that very moment an idea came to me: to have Deaf people teach Hearing people how to improve their communication skills. But was it sound, or even possible? I had never even met a Deaf person in my life. So, I called François:

Bruno: Could I meet two or three Deaf people for a few hours?
François: No problem. Let me see if I have an interpreter available.
Bruno: No. I want to be alone with them. I want to see how it really feels.

Two days later, somewhat apprehensively, I entered a room where three Deaf people were waiting for me. A few hours later I was a different man. Never had I seen people communicate so effectively. They were the role models of communication I had been looking for my whole life. In the following weeks, we observed, compared, and analyzed our two worlds. Working with them, I understood that a handicap is never mental or physical, but behavioral. Truly handicapped people are not those with a malfunctioning body or mind, but those who have developed habits which prevent them from connecting with others in a healthy way. With them, I understood that Deaf people are not deaf when they are together. They become deaf only when they interact with Hearing people. A handicap is never on a person, but on an interaction, which can occur between Hearing and Deaf people as much as within the Hearing world, even if it is less visible. I realized that the real deaf people were Hearing people, their daily misunderstandings and frequent quarrels proving it.

A course was developed where Deaf trainers taught Hearing people how to improve their communication and it became an immediate hit. Hearing participants were shaken to their inner being. Not only could their improvement be measured at the end of a single day of working with Deaf trainers, but because of the emotions they felt, they also remembered long after the lessons what they had learned. Six months after taking such a course, an executive of a high tech company sent me the following message: "The gentle and profound revolution keeps occurring in my mind. Thanks to the Deaf trainers, I have become conscious of how underdeveloped my communication skills were. I have understood that I can improve, and I have learned how to do it. The emotions I felt during the training session deeply affected me, and have given me the desire to change. Thank you for this beautiful lesson in humility."

Thank you Stéphane for having followed your inner voice by writing a name and a phone number on a little piece of paper. Thank you François for having opened the doors of the amazing Deaf world to me.

Interviews

In order to describe communication tips from a Deaf and not a Hearing point of view, each chapter in this book contains numerous transcripts from real Deaf material: face-to-face and virtual interviews.

Face-to-face interviews are real interviews with Deaf people I have met around the globe: in the USA, France, Spain, Italy, China, the UK, and the UAE. These interviews were all conducted with the help of a professional interpreter. Names have been changed in the transcripts to protect the parties' privacy.

Virtual interviews are artificially constructed interviews made out of the raw material of anecdotes found in the autobiographies of Deaf authors, people I have never met. The formulation is my own. Readers who would like to consult the original material will find references in the footnotes.

The deaf person is often in a strong position psychologically.
Either a disability dominates you or you dominate it.
Once it has been dominated it becomes a weapon.
David Wright, Deaf South African Poet

Introduction

Our brain constitutes about 2% of our total body mass but consumes more than 20% of our energy when we are at rest.[123] This means that, proportionally, our major loss of energy is not the result of physical effort, as is often believed, but of mental activities. Not surprisingly, as soon as we wake up, a constant dialogue starts in our head, so intense that it often forces our facial muscles to contract, and our lips to move. Throughout the day, we discuss, argue, and debate with ourselves: "Should I say something?", "Why is he looking at me like that?", "Can't you use your blinker?", "I'm so tired!", "That's an ugly dress!", "He's looking at his watch." "Is there something left in the fridge for tonight?" However hectic we are or deeply we relax, this inner dialogue is continuous. It is even happening to you now as you read these introductory lines. It never stops, except when we start a new dialogue, external this time, to interact with other people. Something we love to do. Not because we wish to exchange information, but because it makes us feel alive.

Just like oxygen, water, or food, interaction with others is a vital need. A human being who is prevented from interacting with other people will simply perish. In his chronicles, Franciscan Salimbene de Parme relates an experiment which was conducted in the thirteenth century by Frederic II of Hohenstaufen. The Holy Roman Emperor wanted to know which language Adam spoke. A crucial question indeed! To find out if it was Hebrew, Latin, or Greek, Frederic II asked several nannies to take care of new born babies without ever talking to them or in front of them. Through this scheme, the Emperor thought that he would discover what language the babies would start to speak naturally. However, the experiment was a complete failure; all the babies died.

Since then, numerous scientific experiments have confirmed that social isolation is indeed detrimental to our psychological and physical health. The solitary confinement of prisoners of war or of criminals causes permanent psychological damage linked to psychosis, depression, and claustrophobia, sometimes pushing people to commit suicide. Statistics show that people who live alone are sick more often and die at an earlier age than married people, even if they are unhappily married. In other words, it is better to have regular interactions with people – even if they are negative – than no interaction at all, the main reason being that we need to be in contact with others to regularly weigh the soundness of our thoughts. If it was not the case, we would quickly disconnect from reality, and become like Alice in Wonderland, dancing lobster quadrilles, and swimming in pools of tears.

That being said, solitary confinement does not occur only in times of war or in prison cells. It can happen to anyone, anywhere: in our homes, schools, and companies. It can happen even when there are people around. Some years ago, when Noam, my eldest son, changed schools, I picked him up at the end of the first day, curious to know how it had gone. My guess was that he had gotten lost in the hallways, or found his new teachers too demanding. But to my surprise, he told me that the most difficult part of the day for him had been the breaks and lunch. How could a playground or a canteen be hard? With much lucidity, he explained to me that during classes, the attention of all the kids, including his own, had been focused on the teacher. But, being new in the school, he had been alone in the playground, and in the cafeteria, while the other kids had gathered in small groups to talk, laugh, and eat together. Breaks and the cafeteria had been harder for him than classes because there he had felt the full weight of isolation. "If I had been just by myself in the playground, or in the cafeteria," he concluded "that wouldn't have been a problem. But to be alone among so many people was real torture."

The ability to communicate with ourselves and with others in a precise, rapid, and respectful way has become one of the most precious skills one can possess today. To acquire it, individuals and companies invest huge sums of money in training, coaching, and therapy. Yet the result is rarely at the level of the investment. Why? Because, as our children show us on a daily basis, three conditions are required to improve: first, a role model to mimic; second, the opportunity to experiment in an environment protected from criticism; and third, pleasure in the learning process.

The most successful programs implement the last two conditions through simulations, games, and exercises run in the safe environment of the training center or the therapy room. But the first condition, the most important, is still missing: a role model to copy. A theoretical model drawn on a board or trainers, acting as if they were good communicators, is not sufficient enough.

Natural role models

Stimulated by their deafness, Deaf people have developed communication skills which enable them to interact with impressive speed and precision beyond those developed by Hearing people.

In a simple exercise, using the work of Hungarian artist Istvan Banyai,[4] participants are placed in groups of three. Each participant randomly receives two pictures from a six image story. Only being allowed to describe what they have in front of their eyes, but without being allowed to show their pictures to the two other members of their team, each group tries to find the correct sequence for each of the six images. To succeed, participants need to understand that the pictures consist of a continuous zoom: a red and yellow plane flying over several islands, one with a volcano. The camera zooms in on the cockpit, where a pilot with a helmet, goggles, and a mike approaches the island. The pilot looks through the cockpit and sees a small group of people on a beach. One of them, the chief of the village, receives a letter from the mailman. Zoom in on the letter, and then zoom in on the stamp which displays a desert landscape with a cowboy watching television. On the next pages follows a word-for-word transcript of both a Deaf group and a Hearing group performing this exercise for the first time. The transcription of the Deaf team was made by recording the voice of a professional interpreter.[5]

Deaf team

[30 seconds of silence. The three participants look at the pictures. Nobody signs]

A: You guys are ready?
B: Yes
C: Yes
A: OK. I have a man in a plane looking towards the left, through a cockpit, at the sea. There is a beach. My second picture is a man in the desert, watching TV. There is the word Arizona written at the bottom of the picture.
B: I also have a picture with a man

Hearing team

[2 seconds of silence. One participant starts talking]

A: I'll go first. One of my pictures displays a desert island, with people holding letters. The other scene is a pilot in a helicopter looking over the beach of a desert island.
B: I have a similar picture. I have a pilot. Maybe a little bit higher up. I can see not only the beach but most of the island's coast. And the other one is one hand holding an envelope with something behind it.

Deaf team

in a plane, also looking towards the left, at the sea. My second image is a man giving a letter to another person.

A: Weird. It seems that our first picture is the same.

C: I see two islands, a sea and a plane. Impossible to see what is inside the plane. The second image is a beach. You can see a family. There is a man with two or three people behind him. They are all black. And there is a mailman. It seems that he is giving a letter to someone.

A to B: What was your second picture again?

B: Someone giving a letter. The people on the beach are indeed black.

C to B: How many people do you see on the beach? A family?

C: No. Only two people. One giving a letter, the other one receiving it.

A to B: You said you had a pilot. I think we have the same picture. Does he have a helmet with a mike?

B: Yes, a red helmet with a yellow strip on the top. I think it's the same picture.

C to A and B: You both have pilots, and I have a plane. It seems as if it's a different point of view. Do you see two islands?

A: No. only one island. Or at least one side of an island, with a beach and four houses on it.

B: I don't see any houses in my picture. But I see a volcano.

A: No volcano in mine. It's more

Hearing team

C: I have two scenes. One is about a plane. It's not very high up but it's still relatively high in the sky. It's overlooking islands but not the coast. My other picture is a cowboy who is sitting next to a cactus and it says Arizona. And he is watching television.

[Long silence]

B: I think your helicopter comes first, my…

A: [Interrupting B talking to C] Can you see several islands?

C: There are no islands at all. I…

A: [Interrupting C] What is he watching?

C: He is watching television.

A: No. Not the cowboy. Your pilot.

C: Oh, my pilot? Islands…

B: [Interrupting C] Several?

C: Several. Yes.

B: So you are high up. I've got a coastline. Some sea. Eeer. A coast line with cliffs and a beach, and you got just…

A: [Interrupting B] The pilot can see the beach and coast, and I've got a horizon line in there.

C: So do I.

A: And he's got his hands on a joystick.

[Long silence]

C: But do you see some coast?

A: I see… Yes. I see a stretch of a beach. Eeeer. Two stretches.

C: I see a wave.

B: I see the coast and houses on it.

C: I see waves.

A: All right. All right.

[A+B+C all speak at the same time. Impossible to decipher the

Deaf team

like a jungle with lots of trees.

C: It's a mysterious island! [laughs]

C to A+B: Is it two different places? What is the shape of the island?

A: There are creeks. The sea is on the right of the beach. Palm trees on the left of the beach.

C: In my picture – the one with someone receiving a letter – there are palm trees behind him, and I think I can distinguish some houses. I am on the island. Not in the air.

A: I think I understand. Maybe the word Arizona on my second picture is on the letter given by the mailman. What do you see on the envelope?

B: Oh yes. You're right. There is a stamp on the letter, and something is written on the stamp. It could be Arizona. In that case, my picture comes before yours.

A: My picture comes after yours.

C: In my picture, the one with a man holding a letter, there are five black guys, and a mailman. The letter is very small.

A: It seems that your picture comes before ours. The mailman gives a letter to someone in a group. There is then a close up on the letter, and then on the stamp.

B: So, the first picture would be the plane with the two islands on the side. The plane flies towards the island where there are houses and people.

B to A: How much of the pilot do you see? I see the pilot from the

Hearing team

recording]

A: So yours is first, mine is second, and you're third.

B: With the pilot?

A: With the pilot! Then, what happens? People are on the beach. There is one hand holding an envelope. You can see it from the back. It's a Black person. And you can see a bit of the detail of the envelope. There are just a few squiggles of writing, and…

B: [Interrupting A] I have a close up of that envelope. I can see the writing with postmark of Arizona to Taumata Tafia, the tribal chief on this island. A Solomon island in Australia.

C: Whereas I have the scene where the cowboy is looking… He is watching television, sitting, with a horse and a trailer. I wonder…

B: [Interrupting C] What is he watching?

C: I wonder… I wonder if he is watching the scene. Yes, I think he is the one actually watching it

B: But what is he watching on the television? Can you see? [Silence]

C: There is some sky, and some rocks. But it is very small. Very small.

A: Do you see the helicopter coming down?

B: Could be.

C: No. No. There is nothing.

A: Nothing you see.

C: No. No.

C: It could be an island. It could be. I mean it could be like a canyon

Deaf team	Hearing team

Deaf team

head to the hands.

A: I only see part of the head and the shoulder. Most of the picture is about the island.

B: So, first the plane in the sky, then a focus on the pilot, then less on the pilot and more on the beach, on the people on the beach, on the letter, and finally on the stamp. Do we all agree?

A+C: Yes.

Hearing team

between two... You know, in a valley. But he's... And he's on his own... And mine says Arizona on it.

B: It says Arizona on it?

C: It says Arizona.

A: Where does it say Arizona?

C: On the right hand side. In the corner.

A: What does it say Arizona on?

C+A: It's just situating it.

C: It's in Arizona.

A: OK. You must be either [B joining] right at the beginning or right at the end.

A: And then we probably have two, three, four, with the... with the pilot.

B: Right.

A: And then mine is the one... Actually it's a postman, now that I look at it, because there is a shoulder bag on the man holding the letter, with mail written on it. And opposite him, there is a very old man with a white beard. He looks like a chief.

B: So...

C: [Interrupting B] Hold on, I have something that I didn't notice before. My plane. I thought it was coming towards. It actually looks like it's leaving. It's either going somewhere or it's coming back.

B: [Sarcastic tone] That's logical!

C: [Embarrassed laugh]: That's all I can say. No... You don't... Because it's passed... It's passed one island on the left... OK! ... And, and going towards another island. You can't tell if it's departing or arriving. Do you see what I'm saying?...

Deaf team	Hearing team
	B: [still sarcastic] Yeah, yeah.
	C: So it could be either the beginning…
	A+B+C: …or the end.
	C: And I… I can't... I don't think it's the end. Because there is one island, that's… That's… You know. Obviously it's… It's passed an island, and then there is another island. I would say he... I would say he's going. He's departing. Because of the water. On the right hand side. It's probably… what do you call them?... One of those water planes, because you can see the trail off. I would say it's departing.
	[Long silence]
	A: What does the man look like?
	A: Long hair, short hair, black hair, white hair?
	C: [Impatient] Black hair. He's got a… It looks like a pony tail. Sitting down. Crossed legs. Red boots. Watching television. Could be dreaming… Could be… Could be… Wait… Could be that what we have is what he is watching.
	A: Television!
	B: Yeah. That's what I…
	C: [Cutting B] Then it would be at the beginning.
	B: But why do we have an envelope? Is it a coincidence that we have an envelope in Arizona… on the Arizona stamp?
	A: And your man is holding a letter?
	B: Yes.
	A: What does he look like?
	B: I can't see.
	A: Does he have white hair, black hair?

Deaf team	Hearing team
	B: It's just… It's just his hand I can see. His hand holding an envelope.
	A: Is he wearing a ring?
	B: No…
	[A+B Talking at the same time.] Incomprehensible.
	A: Any marks on his skin?
	B: No. He is wearing bracelets. He is left handed and is wearing colored bracelets.
	A: Green and yellow?
	B: Green, yellow, blue. And one's got red and white beads on it.
	A: Any of them look like leaves?
	B: No, beads.
	A: Beads?… It's my postman!
	B: Right, so the postman is… He is looking closer at the address.
	A: Yeah.
	B: And then maybe giving it to…
	A: [Interrupting] All right.
	B: Taumata Tafia, the tribal chief.
	A: If my helicopter is coming down…
	C: And my water plane is leaving…
	A: Then, has he dumped letters that the postman has picked up? But what about the cowboy?
	[Long silence]
	C: At the beginning or the end?
	A: Should we make a decision?
	C: [Fed up. Looking nervously at the Deaf team who has finished and is laughing] Let's make a decision!
	A: [placing one picture, face down, on the floor] Here is mine.
	[The others follow reluctantly].

Time: 1 min. 56
Result: No mistake

Time: 6 min. 32
Result: 2 pictures in wrong order

I have conducted this exercise with over 1000 people and the results are always the same. While Deaf people stand in a perfect triangle, close enough to see each other's eyes, far enough apart to see the entire body language of the others, no real pattern can be discerned in the physical positions of Hearing groups. Deaf people look at the pictures in silence before starting to communicate, Hearing people start talking as soon as they receive the pictures. Deaf people place the pictures on the floor, in order to better see the others, and sign more freely. Hearing people talk to the other members of their team with their pictures in front of their faces, rarely making any eye contact. Deaf people describe what they see. Hearing people describe what they imagine. Deaf people never go back to their pictures, as if the image was printed in their brain. Hearing people cannot take their eyes away from the pictures. Deaf people sign for the others, not for themselves. Hearing people don't communicate, they think out loud. Deaf people talk one at a time, in a very sequential manner; Hearing people talk at the same time, and often interrupt each other. Deaf people are simple and precise. Hearing people are either simple and vague, or precise and complex. Deaf people stay focused on the exercise, Hearing people disconnect regularly. Deaf people constantly reformulate and check understanding, saying when they don't understand something. Hearing people never ask others to repeat and never dare to admit that they don't understand. Deaf groups have fun. Hearing groups feel pressure and stress. But most importantly, Deaf groups always succeed in less than two minutes without any mistakes, while Hearing groups regularly have a minimum of one mistake in the sequence, never finish in less than four minutes, more often eight minutes, and sometimes even throw in the towel. Communication is definitely not synonymous with talking.

People often believe that the only difference there is between Hearing and Deaf people is that Deaf people can't hear. This is an over simplistic vision of the world. It would be like saying that the only distinction between Eskimos and Pygmies is the different languages they speak. When we lose one of our senses, we naturally find ways to compensate for that loss.[6] To compensate for their deafness and enhance communication, Deaf people have developed specific behaviors which would be useful to Hearing people… if only they could show some humility. I am always surprised to see that when Deaf people are positioned as a benchmark in communication, some Hearing people get defensive. Sometimes even aggressive. "They can't be all that good!" they say, meaning "We can't be all that bad!" And it is true. I have met Hearing people who were excellent communicators, and Deaf people who were very bad ones. However, this book is not about individuals, but about culture, about strong trends which can be found again and again within specific communities.

The following chapters describe the skills and behaviors which are observed so regularly in the Deaf world that few would challenge the fact that they belong to its culture.

Hearing people can see Deaf people in two different ways: either as people who have lost something – hearing – or as people who have gained something – the ability to communicate without sound. In the first case, Hearing people will express at best compassion towards Deaf people, which will be perceived by them as offensive. In the second case, pity will be replaced by curiosity, respect for the difference, and desire to learn skills which are rarely found in the Hearing world.

Thousands of books and papers have been written on all the sufferings and misfortunes of deafness and on all the things that Deaf people should learn from the Hearing world. This book goes against the tide. Here, the teachers are Deaf people and Hearing people are the students.

How to use this book

In order to prepare yourself for this learning journey, please think about three people with whom you would like your relationship to improve: a family member, a friend, a manager, a team member, a colleague, a client, a supplier, or a neighbor. Open your e-mail or cell phone contact list, or simply think about people you are regularly in contact with. Write their names below.

1. Someone in your close or extended family:

. . . .

2. Someone in your work environment:

. . . .

3. Someone in your social environment:

. . . .

Now, you can launch your 360° Feedback Questionnaire. This questionnaire will help you understand how people see you, and which communication skills you need to develop. At the end of Deaf Tips, you will once again be invited to answer the same questionnaire to measure your progress. In between these two questionnaires, you will find twelve lessons on communication inspired by the Deaf world. These behaviors, tips, and tricks are all interconnected and should be taken as a whole. The chapters of *Deaf Tips* can be read in any order, but please go slowly, allowing yourself to meditate on their teachings, to share with people what you have learned, and to practice the suggested exercises.

We live in a house of mirrors,
and think we look out the window.
Fritz Perls, German Psychiatrist

360° Feedback Questionnaire

We don't see ourselves act. We don't hear ourselves talk. We are not conscious of the impact our words have on people. This lack of awareness often puts us in difficult situations such as speaking too loudly, standing too close, using inappropriate language, concealing emotions, being perceived as arrogant, aggressive, or non-existent. So how can we become more conscious of ourselves to avoid miscommunication? A first step in this direction is to adopt Deaf oralists[7] behavior, using other people as mirrors.

Have you ever wondered how Deaf oralists can learn how to reproduce a sound they have never heard? The process is tedious and often described by them as a via crucis. Day after day, learners place their hand on the throat of their instructors who pronounce specific sounds. By observing their lip movements, the position of the tongue and their muscle contractions, by feeling the vibration of their throat, and the direction and power of the puffs of air escaping their mouth,[8] learners try to replicate what they see, and feel. But as they can't hear what they produce, they must completely rely on the feedback of their speech therapist, and repeat the exercise over and over, each time with minute changes, until they reach the unheard objective. Through this process, they can learn to speak, sometimes, even without the so called *deaf accent*. However, as soon as they stop their speech therapy, and no longer receive feedback, in just a few weeks, their speech regresses until it becomes totally incomprehensible.

This process, which might be somewhat surprising for Hearing people, is however, the very same process the Hearing world uses, even if unconsciously, to speak intelligibly. The only difference being that, instead of going to a speech therapist, Hearing people use their direct environment as mirrors. It is through the constant oral feedback (sorry? excuse me? again? what? huh?) and visual feedback (eyebrows frowning, nose scrunching) they receive that they understand when they have not been clear, forcing them to adapt their speech, often to the point of adopting the same lingo, and sometimes even the same accent as local people.

So it is with behavior. Without regular feedback, we can only behave in a strange way, incomprehensible to other people, not even being aware of it.

A 360° feedback questionnaire is a tool which will help you measure the gap between the way you perceive yourself and the way people see you. Once done, you will be able to identify your major strengths and some potential areas of improvement around twelve communication behaviors. Then, as each of the twelve chapters of *Deaf Tips* corresponds to one of these twelve facets of excellent communication, you will easily understand how to better connect with people, putting into place the tips and tricks suggested by your Deaf teachers. Are you ready? Let's start!

Instructions

1. First, select ten people from your family, social, or professional environment. Select them only if you trust their judgment, and if you are sure that they will have the courage to give you honest feedback on the way you communicate.

2. Make ten photocopies of the following questionnaire, then, place each questionnaire in an envelope.

3. Once the photocopies are done, rate yourself on the 24 questions. To answer, think about real situations you have been in, and be as honest as possible. Write your results below in the book, as it will be more convenient for you to have them at hand whenever you need to refer to them.

4. Once done, approach each of the ten people you have selected, and explain to them your objective: to improve your communication skills. Ask them if they would be willing to answer to 24 questions on the way you communicate. If they agree, give them an envelope.

5. When you receive the results, express your gratitude to the people who answered the questionnaire. And if you have low scores, please don't try to justify yourself. Take the answers for what they are: a perception, a point of view. Not reality.

6. Write down the results – yours and the ones received from the ten people – on the chart following the questionnaire. Observe the discrepancies between the way you see yourself and the way people see

you. What are your strengths? What are your weaknesses? What are the areas on which you all agree, and what are those on which there is a different perception?

7. Keeping the results in mind, you can now read the twelve chapters in the order you wish to, starting with those in which you are the weakest in order to learn how Deaf people succeed in these areas, or with those in which you are the strongest, in order to confirm your rating, and use your strengths as a lever for more improvement.

360° Feedback Questionnaire

Thank you for helping me to improve my communication skills. Please read the following 24 questions carefully, thinking about concrete situations which we have been in together. There is no right or wrong answer. Sometimes you will be tempted to answer the way you wish I had behaved. This is not what is requested here. I would like you to describe how I actually behaved. I want to know what you observe on a regular basis. I need this information to improve. Thank you for your help, and for your honesty.

Scale:
1: I don't know
2: Rarely
3: Sometimes
4: Frequently
5: Always

01	Do I make myself available, and make you feel welcome when we talk?	①②③④⑤
02	Do I take into account the context and the situation, when I try to understand what you say?	①②③④⑤
03	Do I avoid distractions – like looking at my phone or at people walking by – when you talk to me?	①②③④⑤
04	Do I notice facial expressions (e.g., frowning), and react to them ("Let me rephrase, I wasn't clear")?	①②③④⑤
05	Do I avoid technical wording and acronyms with people who don't know them?	①②③④⑤
06	Do I try to see through other people's eyes to feel what they feel, and understand their point of view?	①②③④⑤
07	Do I avoid guessing what you wish to say by interrupting you, and finishing your sentences?	①②③④⑤
08	Do I give you enough time to express what you wish to say without showing signs of impatience?	①②③④⑤
09	Do I use short and simple sentences, avoid getting lost in details and endless explanations?	①②③④⑤
10	Do I adapt my language according to the people I talk to, and the situations I am in?	①②③④⑤
11	Do I know by heart uplifting poems, quotes, or songs, and do I use them regularly?	①②③④⑤
12	Do I prefer positive formulations (yes, can, do), to negative ones (no, can't, don't)?	①②③④⑤

13	Do I admit when I don't know or understand something, and do I readily ask people for help?	①②③④⑤
14	Am I more knowledgeable today than a few months ago? Do I try to learn something new every day?	①②③④⑤
15	Do I concentrate more on what you mean than on what you say?	①②③④⑤
16	Do I pay more attention to you and your needs, when we talk, than to me and what I want?	①②③④⑤
17	Do I often tell stories, relate anecdotes, and use visual and creative language?	①②③④⑤
18	Do I use visual supports such as my body, objects, or drawings, to illustrate what I say?	①②③④⑤
19	Do I remember precisely sentences or stories you told me years ago?	①②③④⑤
20	Do I ever describe important things which happened to you a long time ago?	①②③④⑤
21	Am I comfortable touching people (handshakes, hugs, etc.) when appropriate?	①②③④⑤
22	Do I accept being touched by people (handshakes, hugs, etc.) when appropriate?	①②③④⑤
23	Do I say what I think, even when the environment is hostile?	①②③④⑤
24	Do I say yes when I mean yes, and no when I mean no, instead of using circumlocutions?	①②③④⑤

In your opinion, what are my two major strengths in communication?

1. . . . .

2. . . . .

And what are two areas I should improve to better connect with people?

1. . . . .

2. . . . .

Results

	1	2	3	4	5	6	7	8	9	10	Aver.	Me
Q1												
Q2												
Average for Deaf Tip n°1												
Q3												
Q4												
Average for Deaf Tip n°2												
Q5												
Q6												
Average for Deaf Tip n°3												
Q7												
Q8												
Average for Deaf Tip n°4												
Q9												
Q10												
Average for Deaf Tip n°5												
Q11												
Q12												
Average for Deaf Tip n°6												
Q13												
Q14												
Average for Deaf Tip n°7												
Q15												
Q16												
Average for Deaf Tip n°8												
Q17												
Q18												
Average for Deaf Tip n°9												
Q19												
Q20												
Average for Deaf Tip n°10												
Q21												
Q22												
Average for Deaf Tip n°11												
Q23												
Q24												
Average for Deaf Tip n°12												

In the appropriate boxes, write the results of the ten 360° feedback questionnaires. Q1 to Q24 represent the 24 questions, 1 to 10 the ten people interviewed.

For each of the 24 questions, add up the scores of boxes 1 to 10, divide the result by 10, and write the number in the corresponding average box.

Then, add up the average of Q1+Q2 to discover your average feedback for Deaf Tip n°1. Proceed respectively with Q3+Q4 for Deaf Tip n°2, Q5+Q6 for Deaf Tip n°3, etc.

Once done, write down the score you gave yourself for each question in the column "Me." Add up the scores of Q1+Q2 to discover the score you gave yourself for Deaf Tip n°1. Do the same with Q3+Q4 for Deaf Tip n°2, Q5+Q6 for Deaf Tip n°3, etc.

Finally, below write the 3 most important recommendations you received about improving your communication skills.

1. . . . .

. . . .

2. . . . .

. . . .

3. . . . .

. . . .

Radar chart

The last step: to visualize your results, write the twelve totals you obtained by placing a dot (1 to 10) on the appropriate Deaf Tip axis. Then connect the dots together to create a spider web. Do the same, with a different colored pen, for the twelve totals of your self-assessment.

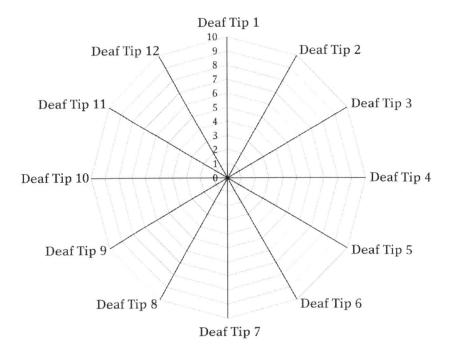

What do you see? Where do the two spider webs overlap? And where do they diverge the most? Do you want to understand why? Do you want to improve? To do it, turn to the corresponding chapters.

Deaf Tip n°1
Prepare to be prepared

Drink the same beverage directly from a can, or from a crystal glass, eat the same meal in front of a TV, or in a cozy restaurant, and the taste will be different. Listen to the same orchestra playing the same piece of classical music on a CD in your living room, or sitting on a pew in an old abbey, watch the same NBA match sitting in the last row, in the first row, or from your sofa, admire the same piece of art in a corporate hall, or in a museum, and again the experience will be different. Read a novel on a tablet, on the recycled paper of a soft cover book, or on the glossy paper of a hard cover one, and even if the novel is the same, the story will have a different echo in you. Step into a cathedral and the walls of stone, the high ceilings, the dim light, and the candles will invite you to murmur. Go to a football stadium, and the colors, the music, and the continuous movement, will push you to shout whatever stupid thoughts come to your mind. Our environment influences the way we capture data, and consequently impacts the way we think, communicate, and behave.

One of the most fascinating experiments on this topic was organized by the Washington Post in 2007. Grammy Award winner Joshua Bell was asked to play the most beautiful pieces of Bach on a Stradivarius worth $3.5 million in a subway station in Washington D.C., while standing next to a garbage can, dressed in a pair of jeans, a t-shirt, and a hat. His 43-minute performance was recorded on hidden camera and then analyzed. The result was dramatic. Out of 1,097 people who walked by, only one recognized the world's greatest violinist and listened to him for about nine minutes. Seven stopped and listened for less than one minute. Twenty-seven gave money, most of them without even stopping to listen. No crowd ever gathered at any time. Nobody ever applauded. Bell, who plays in the most prestigious concert halls with the most famous symphony orchestras, and who makes on average $1,000 a minute, collected $32.17! Whatever their race, gender, or age, every single passer-by saw him as just another beggar.[9]

We all know that the wrapping is often as important as the present. How do you read the symbol in the middle of the illustration bellow? Is it the letter B or the number 13? Clearly, one single symbol cannot be a letter and a number at the same time. Except, of course, if that symbol shares two different environments. Focus on the letter line, and the symbol becomes the letter B. Focus on the number line, and the very same symbol becomes number 13.

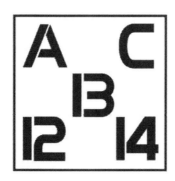

So it is with communication. Sometimes we want to say something important to someone, but it is not the right place, or the right time. And sometimes the setting is perfect, but people are not ready, or available to receive the message. To say what we want to say, and to listen to what is being said – as much as to what is not being said – we need to prepare and be prepared: to prepare our physical environment, and to be prepared psychologically. In these regards, the Deaf world has a few tips to share.

Physical preparation

Have you ever noticed that when you are presented with M&Ms you always choose the same color first? Why do you do it, knowing that they all taste the same? Because colors affect our emotions, and consequently our behavior. Science has proven it. When college students are requested to answer cognitive questions displayed on a red background on a computer screen, they focus on details, avoiding risks. When the same questions are shown on a blue screen, the same students suddenly show more creativity.[10] People believe that orange stimulates appetite, that green gives a feeling of freshness, white of purity and cleanliness, and black of power and authority. Bubble gum pink is used in prisons to calm down aggressive inmates,[11] blue is used in spas to give the feeling of space, peace, and freedom, and red – like the teacher's red pen, or road signs – is used to impress, threaten, or inform about risks or dangers.

Scents, even if imperceptible, also have a strong impact on the way we behave. Divide volunteers into two groups. Ask group A to sit in a room in which a bucket of cleaning solution is hidden. Make sure that the smell of the soap is noticeable but not overwhelming. Place group B – the control group – in a similar room, but without odor. Ask both groups to perform three tasks: First, to write a random chain of words. Second, to write a list of tasks they will do on the next day. Third, to eat cookies. The result is stunning. For the first task, group A uses more words related to cleaning than group B. For the second task, group A plans more washing and tidying up than group B. And for the third task, group A cleans up three times more of the cookies crumbs on the table than group B.[12]

Like Hearing people, Deaf people are influenced by colors and scents. But contrary to Hearing people, they are very conscious, and consequently more sensitive about how the setting of our physical environment impacts our communication.

Lew: Like that snack bar close to my office which looks noisy.
Bruno: Why do you say that it *looks* noisy?
Lew: Because the walls and the floor are tiled, the ceiling is high, the lights are bright and it's always crowded, often with teenagers. Whenever I go there, I always tend to raise my voice as if I was in a loud place, until someone asks me to turn down the volume.
Bruno: Interesting. And do you know places which *look* quiet?
Lew: Of course. Places like restaurants with dim lights, dark walls, or walls covered with fabric, with a thick carpet on the floor and very few customers. When I'm in such an environment I automatically start whispering. It's often appropriate. But sometimes it also happens that people tell me that they can't hear me because loud music is blasting from speakers hidden above my head.[13]

The way the furniture is arranged impacts the way we communicate. Benches in railway stations, chairs lined up in waiting rooms, and rows of chairs in a classroom discourage people from talking, while tables and chairs positioned in a circle or in a square on the terrace of a café, or in a cozy restaurant, encourage people to converse, to share, and to connect.

Think about the following situations: (1) you want to help your child to do his or her homework; (2) you want to have a casual conversation with a friend; (3) you want to give a warning to a team member who challenges your authority; (4) you don't want to talk to a stranger. For each situation, which of the following settings would you instinctively choose?

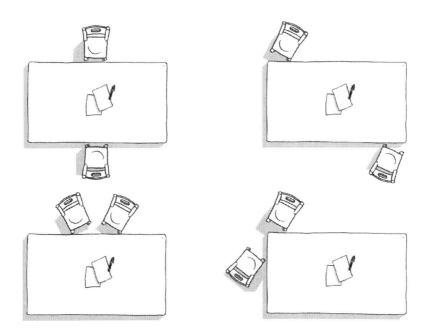

According to Sommer,[14] people who want to converse, naturally tend to sit at the corner of a table. When they want to collaborate, they sit on the same side, preferably on the long side of the table. And when they come with a spirit of competition or contention, they sit on opposite sides of the table, preferring again the length of the table, facing one another, eye to eye. If the table is round, the situation is less visible, but nevertheless similar. People who sit next to each other tend to converse and collaborate. People who have opposing views tend to take opposing seats.

Unconsciously, we always choose a place which best reflects our state of mind, be it with a seat, the table, or in the room: in our office when we want to use power over a team member, at their job station when we want to give them recognition, and at the coffee machine for a more neutral discussion. Similarly, in our private life, we sit on the kids' bed for a personal chat, in the living room for a family counsel, around the kitchen table for a casual talk.

Deaf people do the same, except that when they do it, to improve the quality of communication, they specifically and consciously take three physical criteria into consideration: light, distance, and noise, adapting them if needed. Let's start with the first criteria: light.

Julia: The first thing I check when I enter a room is the quality of light. Is it natural or artificial? Direct or indirect? Frontal or from the back? Depending on what I find, I either sit down, relax, and enjoy the conversation, or change seats, close a curtain, or turn a light on, until I find the visual comfort I'm looking for.

Bruno: Why so much effort?

Julia: Because when you talk with people who are standing in front of a window during the daytime, or directly under a light, they have shadows on their face.

Bruno: And?

Julia: And these shadows don't allow me to have a precise reading of their body language. And if I can't see them correctly, I can't understand them correctly.

Bruno: So, too much light isn't good?

Julia: That's right. But not enough is even worse.

Do you trust people who say: "Trust me"? Not always? Why? And when your work is complimented with a "Well done!" do you take it as encouragement or as harsh criticism? How is it possible to interpret the very same words in different ways? When someone says "I love you" do you believe them? We react to people's intentions, and their intentions are never found in the words they say, and rarely in their tone of voice, but always in their body language. This is even truer when there is a discrepancy between what they say, the way they say it, and what their body is expressing. In such cases, like everybody else, our instinct forces us to trust the body first, the tone of voice second, and then, only last, the words.

On this topic, Bateson tells an interesting story about a young man who was recovering from schizophrenia, and who was visited by his mother at the hospital. The young man was glad to see his mother "… and impulsively put his arm around her shoulders, whereupon she stiffened. He withdrew his arm and she asked "Don't you love me anymore?" He then blushed, and she said "Dear, you must not be so easily embarrassed and afraid of your feelings" […] Following her departure [the young man] assaulted an aide and was put in the tubs."[15]

To understand people, to capture not only what they say, but more importantly, what they mean, and what their real intention is, we need to read their body language correctly. At home, at work, or in your social life, apply this Deaf strategy: reposition the furniture if necessary to avoid talking to people with light behind them, or directly above their head. Prefer natural to artificial light, and if not possible, invest in comfortable indirect lighting if you can.

The second criteria Deaf people take into account to improve communication is distance. Deaf people always try to get close to the people they want to interact with. A shocking behavior in a world where people tend to communicate more and more by sms or e-mail, even with colleagues or friends who are just a few meters away.[16] Of course, this is not to say that electronic communication should be prohibited. These tools are useful, but they will never replace, or attain the quality of face-to-face interactions. Misunderstandings and conflicts increase with electronic communication, and decrease with face-to-face interaction. Except if despite the proximity you don't or can't look the other person in the eyes.

Bonnie: For as soon as you lose eye contact, things can really go wrong. But of course, only Deaf people can understand this.
Bruno: What do you mean? Why only Deaf people?
Bonnie: One day, in a restaurant, I went to the ladies' room. When I left the stall, and went to the sink to wash my hands, I saw a lady coming out of the stall next to the one I had used. She looked mad. I saw her open my stall, take a look inside, and then walk towards me shouting.
Bruno: Could you read on her lips what she was saying?
Bonnie: I think it was something like: "You b.....! There are two rolls of toilet paper in your stall. Why didn't you pass me one when I asked you?"
Bruno: Did you tell her that you were Deaf?
Bonnie: No. I didn't have the time. Before I was able to explain that I couldn't have heard her request, she had already stormed out of the ladies' room, slamming the door.[17]

Nothing will ever replace a direct, face-to-face interaction… as long as you know where to stand, of course. Too far apart and you can't connect. Too close and people will be uncomfortable.

According to Hall,[18] people need at least 120 cm of space around them to feel at ease in a public environment. But as soon as they are with people they know, the distance shortens to about 45 cm, in order not only to see, but also to smell, and feel the body heat of the other person, even if it is unconsciously.[19] If these unspoken codes are broken, an odd dance begins with one person getting closer, the other stepping back, the first getting closer again, the second stepping back again, leading sooner or later to a fight or flight outcome. Not fully convinced? Sit next to someone you don't know in an empty bus and observe how your neighbor quickly shows signs of discomfort, feeling threatened, even if he or she is unable to really explain why. Now do it again, with the same traveler, but this time in a bus which is crowded. Sit next to the same person, and he or she will not even notice your presence. Same people, same seats, different reactions.

Deaf people apply a similar code of conduct. They always stop about 150 cm from the people they want to communicate with. The reason, however, is not to respect the private sphere described by Hall, but to improve communication. For a one-to-one interaction 150 cm is the ideal distance one needs to be close enough to see the pupil, iris, sclera[20] and facial muscle contractions with precision, and at the same time far enough away to be able to capture the rest of the body language (e.g. nervous gestures of the legs and feet). Closer than that and you miss body language information. Farther than that and you lose facial expressions. Once you are comfortable with this distance for one-on-one interactions, the next step is to adapt it to the group. Can you recall a time when you wanted to get involved in a group discussion and the circle did not open to you? Do you remember the feeling?

Myron: When I was a child, my parents often took me to the beach. The ritual was always the same. When we arrived there were already two or three Deaf couples sitting on beach chairs in a circle. As soon as they saw us come, they would expand the circle to welcome us in. And all morning, as additional Deaf people arrived...

Bruno: ...the circle would open?

Myron: Yes. Every time a Deaf family arrived, conversations stopped, beach chairs and umbrellas were repositioned to enlarge the circle, and then, hands flew again to resume their conversation where they had left off. This would happen over and over again

Bruno: How big could the circle be?

Myron: By 4 o'clock, when everyone had arrived, there was at least one hundred beach chairs positioned in a perfect circle with Deaf people signing to one another, sometimes to people right across the circle.

Bruno: Not very discreet...

Myron: Indeed. But you know, because of the nature of our language, there are very few secrets in the Deaf community [laugh].[21]

I have observed this Deaf behavior again and again. It is seen for example in Deaf schools where seating arrangements are not in rows like in Hearing classrooms, but circular to allow everyone to see and be seen. And so it is during informal discussions. Hearing people believe that they can communicate without looking at each other, walking side by side, talking with their backs turned, or even talking from another room. This would never happen in the Deaf world. Deaf people always make sure that anyone who is involved in a discussion has visual access to the person who is signing, because they know that the key to understanding each other is not in the words or in the signs, but in the body language of the person who is talking.

Below is a visual representation of how Hearing people position themselves when they talk:

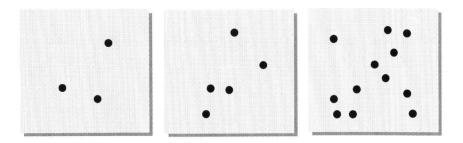

The difference between the Deaf and the Hearing world becomes very visible as soon as three people are involved in a conversation. Three Deaf people will position themselves in a perfect equilateral triangle. Three Hearing people will form at best an obtuse triangle. And as the number of participants increases, the shape becomes more and more precise in the Deaf world, and more and more undefined in the Hearing one. So, if you want to improve the quality of communication when you are talking in a group, it might be useful to review your geometry lessons.

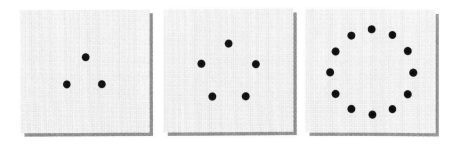

When there are three of you, position yourselves in a triangle. When there are four, create a square. It is easy. More difficult, now. When there are five, position yourselves in a pentagon. Six? In a hexagon. Fourteen? In a tetrakaidecagon. Thirty-seven? In a triacontakaiheptagon. And if you don't remember all these words, then you have only two choices: either you limit your group conversations to four people, or you simply create a circle which you expand as people join in and reduce as they leave, in order to always keep an equal distance between the people involved in the discussion. As a result, everyone will feel more welcome, and will be able to better understand others, as they will have access not only to their words, but more importantly, to their body language.

The third physical criterion to improve the quality of communication is noise. When Deaf people choose a place to communicate they take noise into account. Aural noise for hard of hearing people, visual noise for Deaf people.

Josh: It was so easy for me to communicate with people when I was living in Mununga, a small village of Zambia, Africa.
Bruno: How could you find communication easier with people who didn't speak your language?
Josh: Oh, it was not so much about people than about the place. I was living in a nice flat open village. There was no background noise. Only the pleasant hush of the river. No cars passing by. No TV or radio. No phones. Not all those beeping electric appliances we have in the USA which reduces our ability to understand the other so much.[22]

This is true for the hard-of-hearing, as much as it is for Hearing people. Before you start talking, or when you really want to listen to other people, close the window if there is noise outside, turn the video projector, the TV, your phone, or the radio off, ask people to refrain from side conversations, and then enjoy the quality of the discussion. And in the case of unexpected noise – e.g., a plane flying overhead or a truck driving by – just stop talking, and use the time to clarify and structure your thoughts. What do you want to say? Why do you want to say it? And what is the most appropriate way of saying it?

This is true for aural noise as much as it is for visual noise. Studies show that people who work on a clean desk increase their ability to understand complex data by 12%. People who work in a messy environment reduce it by 24%. Why? Because our brain can't avoid analyzing everything which is in its field of vision, even when it is not requested to: What is written on that piece of paper? Why is the LED on my phone blinking? Who left a message? What is the message about? Who is that person who just walked by? And all the energy that our brain burns in dealing with this noise cannot be used to understand anything else.

If you are on the terrace of a café and you want people to listen to you, select a seat whose back is to a wall to avoid visual noise behind you. You want to pay attention to your son who is talking to you? Turn away from your computer or from the television. Having worked for so long with Deaf people, today, I cannot talk with people anymore when there is an obstacle in my field of vision, even if it is a simple bottle of water on the table. I have to remove it, and I believe that in doing so it considerably improves our ability to communicate.

Psychological preparation

Once you are comfortable with your physical environment: colors, smell, furniture, light, distance, and noise, the last step to prepare yourself for powerful communication is in your head. Before opening your mouth, for a few minutes, look around, observe people, read their body language, analyze their behavior. How do they feel? What do they think? What do they say? What do they want?

David: As I'm Deaf, I can't afford to take my eyes away from people when I'm interacting with them, not even for a few seconds to look at what's going on around me. If I did, I would quickly lose track of the conversation.
Bruno: So, how do you remain attuned to your environment?
David: Oh, for that I've developed a technique. A Deaf tip which I'm sure could also help Hearing people.
Bruno: What is it?
David: When you arrive in a place where people are talking: stay on the sidelines for a while. Don't jump into a conversation right away. Take a few minutes to observe the place, the people, their mood. Absorb as much information as possible. Then you can interact with people. By doing so, you will be able to focus more on the conversation, without having to constantly check around you to see what is happening, looking at something else other than the person who is talking to you.[23]

By adopting this good practice, you will know what to expect, and consequently always be ready to react in an appropriate way.

Lew: When I was a student, one night my Hearing roommates went out for dinner to a nearby fast food restaurant. As I was preparing for an exam, I didn't go with them. But one hour later, as they had not yet returned, I went to the restaurant to join them.
Bruno: Did you find them?
Lew: Yes. The restaurant was crowded but after a few seconds, I found them in a corner, around a table. They had finished their dinner and were chatting. No doubt that they would leave soon.
Bruno: And I suppose you were hungry.
Lew: No. Not really. But a waitress came up to me, from behind, and asked me if I wanted to order something. I didn't see her come, I didn't see her stand behind me, and of course I couldn't see her lips movement. But still, I turned around and politely said "Nothing, thank you." My roommates who all knew that I was completely deaf were shocked.

Bruno: They should have been! How did you know that the waitress was behind you, asking you something, if you couldn't see her?

Lew: Because before sitting down I had seen her at a nearby table, and because just before answering, I had felt small puffs of air on my neck, a sure sign that someone was talking to me from behind me.

Bruno: Incredible. But how did you know that she was asking you if you wanted to order something?

Lew: What else do you think a waitress would ask in such a situation?

Bruno: I'm impressed!

Lew: Well, it's in fact quite simple to react in an appropriate way when you know what to expect.[24]

Emerson said that we only hear what we are ready to hear, and see what we are prepared to see. When Noam, my oldest son, was taking lessons for his driving license, I started thinking about what type of car I could buy him. One day, as I was driving home I thought that a good first car might be a Mehari. The Mehari was a beach car produced in 1968 by Citroen, a French car manufacturer. It was a two-seater, with the body made out of plastic, easy to drive, easy to repair. It was very trendy in the seventies. When I was at University, one of my friends had one, and everyone saw him as being so cool. I thought that this would be a good choice for a first car, despite the fact that it would be very difficult to find one in good condition as production had stopped in 1987. As I was thinking about this, a Mehari pulled up in front of me, which brought a big smile to my face. Was it a sign from Heaven? I don't think so. I could have come across ten Meharis on the previous day, and I would not have seen them. It is because I was thinking at that very moment about this specific car that I saw it. It reminded me that when Magali, my wife, was pregnant, it seemed to me at the time that every woman I came across was pregnant too.

It is impossible to see or hear something that we have not imagined first. We can see and hear in the real world only what we have been able to project first in our mind's eye. We don't believe what we see. We see what we believe.

Lew: This is the reason why at the office, at home, in a bus, on a plane, or in the toilets, I always need something close at hand to read: a tablet, a book, a magazine, a newspaper… even a cereal box.

Bruno: I don't understand.

Lew: We must read a lot to be as knowledgeable as possible because the more we read, the more we know. And the more we know, the more we are able to cope with about any type of conversation or situation.[25]

The more knowledge we acquire in life, the more able we are to see, hear, and understand. The more information we gather on topics as diverse as possible, the more able we are to transform abstract data into concrete meaning. It is knowledge and experience which help us turn a closed situation into multiple opportunities. Children under the age of eight see a man and a woman dancing in the picture below. Sometimes they see the head of an owl or of a crow. What about you? What do you see?

Deaf Tip n°1: Prepare to be prepared
Exercises

- Teaching others is the best way to learn. Share something you have learned in this chapter with at least three friends, colleagues, or members of your family.
- Think about where you spend most of your time (office, living room, kitchen, bedroom, etc.) What could you do to improve the color, the furniture set up, or the lighting? How could you reduce aural and visual noise?
- Stand up and move to the other side of your desk when someone comes to see you. Place a chair next to your desk to make people feel comfortable if they want to have a chat with you.
- Turn your phone off, move away from your computer, avoid looking at your watch or at people walking by when you interact with someone.
- Buy essential oils to make your office and your house smell inviting, relaxing, and warm. Place a few drops on the filter of your vacuum cleaner to perfume your house when you clean it. Sow patches of mint in your lawn, so when you mow you will enjoy the smell.
- As you talk with people you regularly interact with, slowly get closer to them until you see that they feel uncomfortable, then move slowly away from them until you feel that you disconnect. Then, remember the ideal distance that each person expects from you.
- Learn something new this month. Read a book about something you don't know about (business, sport, architecture, science, etc.), start piano or drama lessons, or learn a new language – why not Sign Language? Use stumbleupon.com to discover websites you have never visited before.
- Before starting any serious conversation with someone or with a group, take a few minutes to observe yourself as much as the others, and ask yourself the following questions: What is your level of energy? Are people psychologically available? How do they feel? What do they think? What is the message you want to pass on? What is the message they expect to hear? Then, adapt your message and your language to what you have perceived.
- What could you do to improve your communication with the three people you selected in the introduction?
- Practice, practice, practice.
- Once done, move on to another chapter.

Personal Notes

Deaf Tip n°2
Read body language

It is deceptive to call Hearing people *hearing* and Deaf people *deaf*. Why would a group of people be labeled by an attribute they have, and the other by one they don't have? This is discriminatory, and misleading. If we really wanted to precisely describe Hearing and Deaf people based on the sense they use the most, the two communities would respectively be called *Talking* and *Seeing* people.

Emilie: When I was five, my parents took me to New York. We went to Charles de Gaulle Airport with a huge red suitcase, checked-in, and got on the plane. Once we landed in New York, we went to baggage claim to pick up our luggage. We found the right belt and waited. There were a lot of people waiting with us. Finally the belt was activated and luggage started to arrive. As my dad picked up a big red suitcase, I told him that it was not ours.
Bruno: Not yours?
Emilie: No. I had noticed that our suitcase had a small defect on one of the two locks, a two millimeter gap, and it was not the case on this one.
Bruno: How did your dad react?
Emilie: He smiled at me, picked up the suitcase, and put it on the trolley.
Bruno: And?
Emilie: And, I insisted. I knew it was not our suitcase. But he still took it. After all, the suitcase was big, red, and I was only five. What did I know?
Bruno: I bet you were panicked.
Emilie: I certainly was, especially when my dad started to walk away. But then, at that very moment, another big red suitcase landed on the belt. It was the exact same one. I pulled the sleeve of my dad's coat, and pointed at the suitcase on the belt. My parents saw it, and suddenly had a doubt. My dad checked the tag, and discovered that I was right. They were leaving with someone else's suitcase [laugh]. They were so impressed by my ability to see details that even today, more than twenty years later, they still talk about it.

Active observation can help us find the right suitcase, but more importantly, it can help us better understand people. It is not by asking questions that we get to know people, it is by carefully observing them in their environment. The way they talk in front of their family, colleagues and friends, and the way they talk when they are gone, the way they dress and decorate their house, the books they buy, and those they read, the food they eat, and how they eat it, and of course the way they move their body, reveal who they are better than any description they could give of themselves. To know and to understand people, we have to listen with our eyes, not with our ears.

Savanah: I grew up in a small village in Morocco. As I was deaf, instead of going to school, I sat all day long with my Mom at the market – she sold things there – and my favorite pastime was to observe people. I quickly discovered that I could tell how people felt, and the type of relationship they had one with another, and I often shared this with my Mom.
Bruno: How would she react?
Savanah: She would tell me that I had too much imagination, and that I should not make up stories. But she soon had to change her mind.
Bruno: Why?
Savanah: There was a woman who came to the market every day. Everyone knew her. She was very pleasant. But one day, as she was walking by, I noticed that something had changed.
Bruno: What?
Savanah: She was still smiling and being nice to everyone, but it wasn't like before. It was as if she was wearing a mask now. She was hiding something. She was sad, or maybe afraid. I remember I thought she was being mistreated by someone.
Bruno: Did you tell your Mom?
Savanah: As usual [smile]. But when I told her, she would not believe me. But the more I observed this woman, the more I was convinced that something was wrong. I kept on telling my Mom that that lady was suffering. Finally, my mother decided to talk to her.
Bruno: And?
Savanah: The lady had been married for just a few weeks. She was being abused by her husband, and nobody knew it. Thanks to my observation skills, my mother, who had a lot of influence in the village, was able to help her.

Contrary to what most people believe, we don't communicate as much with our words – or signs – as with our face, something I experienced first-hand with Deaf people. One day, my Sign Language teacher arrived with one hand wrapped up in bandages. I was surprised that despite the accident he had had, he had still come to teach me. So, I tried my first Deaf joke on him. I signed: "Would it be correct to say that a Sign Language teacher who has both hands in a cast is aphonic?" He smiled, and then, to make me pay for my insolence, he closed his other hand and gave the whole lesson with two stumps. My first reaction was to panic. My second was to focus more than ever on his face. And to my great surprise, at the end of the lesson, despite the lack of hands and fingers, I had understood everything.

Why is the face such an incredible source of information? Because despite our culture, gender, or age, despite all of the efforts we make to control our body, our emotions constantly pop up at the surface of our skin, in micro-movements, contracting a muscle here, relaxing another there, causing an eyebrow to raise slightly, an eye to narrow a little, or a corner of the mouth to drop faintly. We just can't help it. It is nearly impossible to stop an expression from appearing on our face, and very difficult to fake one.[26] Muscle contractions and changes in the color of our skin are the crystallization of our emotions. And as emotions are universal,[27] by practicing active observation, we have access to the emotions of any human being, and consequently to their thoughts. And if we don't notice this more often, it is simply because we all have a strong tendency to focus more on ourselves than on others.[28]

Before my first visit to India, I was told that when Indians shake their head from right to left, it doesn't mean that they disagree, just that they are thinking. A few days later, in New Delhi, armed with this new cultural knowledge, I entered a training room full of Indians. After only a few minutes, fifteen heads started to shake from right to left. I repeated to myself: *They don't disagree, they are thinking. They don't disagree, they are thinking.* But despite this mental mantra, they kept on shaking their heads from right to left. Finally, I couldn't stand it anymore. I stopped the training session, and asked: *Any problem with what we have seen so far?* A useless question if I had been paying more attention to them than to myself, if I had really looked at their facial expressions, instead of focusing on my own little beliefs and patterns. When we make the effort to carefully observe other people's faces, we suddenly realize that their thoughts are indeed visible.

Emmanuelle: When I was a child, I just couldn't understand how people could talk without looking at each other. They would do it with their backs turned to one another, or even from another room. It was a mystery to me. Personally, I could understand people only when they showed me their face.

Bruno: And what was your reaction when people turned their back to you while talking?

Emmanuelle: I would pull their clothes, or even take their head in my little hands and place it in front of mine, meaning: Look at me. Show me your face so I can understand what you're telling me.

Bruno: This is clearly a Deaf way: to look at the other person's face when talking. Why do you think Hearing people don't do this?

Emmanuelle: I've no clue. Even animals know about the importance of looking at each other's face to communicate better.

Bruno: Animals? What do you mean?

Emmanuelle: I had a black cat who knew I was deaf.

Bruno: How do you know that your cat knew that you were deaf?

Emmanuelle: Oh, it's quite simple. When he was hungry or thirsty he would simply meow. My mother would hear him, find him, and then bring him food or water.

Bruno: And with you?

Emmanuelle: With me, I guess he tried to do the same, but as I couldn't hear him, he had to adapt to the situation if he wanted to eat. He quickly understood that the best way to get what he wanted with me was to meow in my face. He knew that to be heard he had to force eye contact, to dive his beautiful green eyes deep into mine.

Bruno: Why can't Hearing people do this?

Emmanuelle: I don't know if it's a lack of energy or a lack of courage, but indeed, they rarely look each other in the face.[29]

Can we become, like Deaf people, better observers of our environment, better observers of other people? And if we were to try, what should we focus on? To find out, look at the four faces below. Which one makes you feel the most uncomfortable?

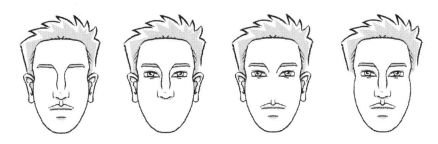

To this question, 63% of people answer that it is the face without eyes which makes them feel the most uncomfortable, 18% the one without a mouth, 11% without ears, and only 8% without a nose.[30] In other words, when we look at a face, more than 80% of the people focus only on the eyes and on the mouth, ignoring the rest of the face.

One day, I decided to shave my goatee. But as soon as I did it, I regretted it. It looked like someone had chopped my jaw off. What would my clients say? Would my colleagues make fun of me? I went to work reluctantly, feeling apprehensive before each encounter. But to my great surprise no one made any comment. I first thought that people were being very polite, and I expected less solicitude from my family. When I went home that night, I was ready for a good laugh around the dinner table. But again, not one single comment was made. I didn't say a word; I wanted to know how long it would take for people to notice the change. Yet, after a few days, my initial feeling of embarrassment turned into irritation. I was shaving every morning, sometimes even in front of my wife, but still, no comment. Feeling frustrated, I decided to probe people:

"Have you noticed anything different about me?"
After a long silence, and after having observed every square millimeter of my body, the answer was always the same:
"No, what?"
"I shaved my goatee!"
"Oh, that's right… I knew something had changed, but I didn't know what. When did you do it? This morning?"
"No. I did it a week ago…"

It didn't concern my eyes, or my mouth, so it was invisible. For people, a human face consists only of two eyes and one mouth. This is so true that when you double the number of eyes and mouth on a face, people get confused. They don't know on which pair of eyes or on which mouth they should focus, their eyes move non-stop from one pair to the other. A reaction which would be completely different if it was the ears which had been doubled.

Same if you turn a face upside down, while keeping the eyes and the mouth in the normal position. Despite the fact that only a small percentage of the surface of the face is in the right position – the eyes and the mouth – everything seems more or less normal. But, if you do the opposite, placing the face in the right position while inverting only the eyes and the mouth (turn the book upside down), suddenly, the very same face turns ugly. This shows, once again, how important the eyes and the mouth are for people.

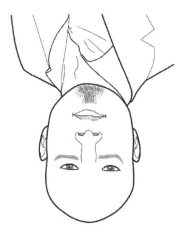

When presented with these statistics and experiments, Deaf people are not surprised. They know that most of the information which is needed in communication is not found in sound waves, words, or signs, but in the micro movements which can be observed on, in, and around the mouth and the eyes. The eyes and the mouth are definitively the most important places to capture information about others, and there is an order to follow: first the eyes, then the mouth.

The eyes are the nipples of the face[31]

After only five hours, infants show a preference for looking at their mother's face.[32] After two days, they are able to recognize their mother's face from that of someone else. After four weeks, babies spend about 20% of their waking time scrutinizing their mother's face. And when they are nine weeks old, they spend 90% of their time looking at their mother's eyes, even if the mother is talking, or moving her hands, which shows that babies look at the eyes not because they are moving, but because they are eyes.[33] Many researchers have conducted experiments, placing highly schematized face-like shapes, such as two big circles, one with two dots in the middle, the other one empty, in front of babies' eyes. Without exception, babies spend more time scrutinizing the circle with the two dots than the one without *eyes*.[34] This is an attraction which we still feel years later. Try it. Take a piece of paper, and draw an oval on it. Add a mouth, a nose, and two ears, but don't draw the eyes yet. Don't worry if you aren't a great artist. Look at the picture carefully. How do you feel? Now, pay attention to your feelings as you draw two simple dots where the eyes should be. Do you notice how these two small dots suddenly make you feel better by simply reflecting your own look?[35]

Esther: Eyes are so important for Deaf people!
Bruno: More than their lips? Don't you read on lips?
Esther: If you talk to me while covering your mouth with your hand, I can still understand you, but if you talk while covering your eyes, you suddenly become silent to me, even if you move your lips.
Bruno: So you don't read lips?
Esther: No. In fact not many Deaf people read lips.
Bruno: Well, in any case, I guess that there are not a lot of people talking with their hand over their mouth or over their eyes [laugh].
Esther: More than you think [smile]. Deaf people have a hard time understanding people who have a beard or a moustache which covers their lips, but they simply can't understand people who wear dark sunglasses.
Bruno: Why is that?
Esther: Because it is only by looking in people's eyes that you can understand their intentions. Information you can't get anywhere else.
Bruno: Are you saying that if we paid less attention to people's words and more to their eyes, we would understand them better? Is that what you do?
Esther: That's right.

Some years ago, I was part of a European delegation visiting Asia, meeting government representatives and captains of industry to promote industrial cooperation. After visiting a few countries, the colleague I was teamed up with made the remark that we always went faster than any of the other teams, sometimes finishing our interviews and report one day before the others. Was it because we were so good, or because we wanted so much to have time to visit the country? To find out, we decided to pay more attention to what was happening. By listening to our colleagues, we realized that, despite the fact that they had learned all the dos and don'ts in intercultural awareness courses, the words many of them used to describe Asian people were extremely offensive. This triggered our curiosity. Could people detect their real thoughts behind all the positive words and behaviors they were using? My colleague and I loved Asian cultures, and had not taken any intercultural classes. We decided to try a little experiment, using Deaf magic. The next country we were to visit was Bhutan, a highly enigmatic place for Westerners. During the trip to Bhutan, we listened carefully to our colleagues and wrote down all the recommendations they gave to one another, and we decided to do the exact opposite. We would do the exact opposite, but at the same time we would look people deep in the eyes, thinking intensely about the love and respect we had for them and for their culture, and about our strong desire to help them and work with them. On that visit, despite the fact that we did everything wrong – no ritual greeting, no business card exchanged with two hands, etc. – we finished two days before any other team, and were the only one to be invited by a family to share dinner. When you really look in people's eyes, you understand who they are. However, before doing so, you need to ask yourself a crucial question: do you really want to know?

Myron: That's right. When you really look at a person's face, it can completely change the way you see them, and consequently the relationship you have with them. I believe I can capture more information in a slight muscle contraction around someone's eyes than my brothers and sisters – who are hearing – can when they listen to a one hour conversation.
Bruno: You're a bit hard on them, aren't you?
Myron: No. It's the truth. Let me give you an example. When we are at my father's house, I often see my mother-in-law looking at my father as if he was a spider coming out of a cupboard. I can see in her eyes how much she would like to smash him like an insect.
Bruno: Nice lady! And you are the only one to see that?
Myron: Yes. It seems that I'm the only one. My brothers and sisters still believe that she loves our father. They are blinded by her words. But you can't fool a Deaf person with words. We see the truth in people's eyes.[36]

Contrary to Deaf people, Hearing people believe that they can interact without looking at the other person. Sometimes they do it for hours. In some cases, they find it easier because the subject is sensitive or intimate. However, it is not because it is easier that it is more efficient. Would you prefer someone who says *I'm sorry* or *I love you* while looking you in the eyes or avoiding eye contact? If your emotions are positive, and if what you say matches what you think, then eye contact is the only way to build trust, and encourage people to open up.

Lew: Hearing people can't keep eye contact for more than a few seconds. More than that and they start to look very uncomfortable. I guess that's the reason why they so often break eye contact to look somewhere else.
Bruno: And does it bother you?
Lew: For Deaf people eye contact is extremely important. When someone doesn't look at me when I talk it gets on my nerves, but I accept it when it's cultural.

Bruno: What do you mean when it's cultural? It's not always cultural?
Lew: No. Sometimes it's not a problem of culture, but of education, or even worse, of a lack of respect for others. Like those people who have that irritating habit of constantly letting their eyes wander around to look at everything except you. Their eyes are like radar scanning their environment without interruption, desperately looking for something more interesting than you and what you're saying.
Bruno: And I empathize. I really hate it when I talk to people who are playing with their phone or looking at people walking by at the same time. But what about the opposite? Being Deaf, you look more intensely in people's eyes, more intensely than they are used to. Does it bother them?
Lew: I've never gotten this comment. On the contrary, the feedback I always get is that people are flattered by the way I concentrate on their face when they talk, which for them means: "What you say is important. You're important to me."[37]

Much research confirms that there is indeed a strong correlation between our eye contact and the influence we have on people. Chris Kleinke, professor of psychology at the University of Alaska, has demonstrated in a series of experiments that when you leave coins in a phone booth, and ask the person who used the phone right after you for the money you *forgot*, you have an 86% chance of getting the money back if you look the person straight in the eyes, but only a 72% chance if you avoid eye contact. Similarly, beggars receive more money, waitresses more tips, and hitchhikers more lifts, when they also look people straight in the eyes.

This is a trick that many charismatic people know and use. Hitler, for example, who needed glasses, never wore them during public speeches. He believed that the glasses would disrupt the connection between him and his audience. His speeches were scripted only in headlines and in half-inch type. When delivering a speech, Hitler would always use the same pattern for each paragraph. He would first start in a moderate manner, raising the tone in the middle of a sentence, and finishing with a roar. He would then raise his right hand with the fingers lifted for the *Zich Heil*, and while the crowd would scream the same, he would quickly look at the next headline on the paper in his left hand, ready for the next paragraph. In doing so, Hitler never lost eye contact with the crowd when talking, consequently increasing his control over the people.[38] Eye contact links people, both in terms of influence and allegiance. In fact, by simply observing the direction, the duration, and the intensity of the eye contact people exchange in a room, it is easy to find out who is in power, even if not one single word has been uttered. In life, the person in a group who looks at the most people, and, at the same time, who receives the highest number of looks (in the example below: Lily) is, without any doubt, the leader of the group, even if no one is conscious of it, and even if it doesn't correspond to the official organizational chart or to what is written on people's business cards. It is not you, but the relationship you have with people which defines who you are. In a theater play, the king is the king because everybody bows in front of him. Not because he wears a crown or believes that he is king. So it is in real life.

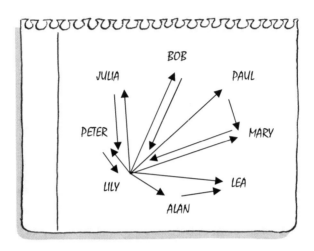

And of course, the more precise your eye contact is, the more powerful and effective your connections with other people will be.[39] For this, once again, Deaf people are a benchmark for the Hearing world. When conversing, Deaf people never use each other's names. While Hearing people would say: "Hello Paul, how are you?" Deaf people sign: "Hello, how are you?" While Hearing people would say: "Mary, can you pass me the salt, please?" Deaf people sign: "Can you pass me the salt, please?" This specific behavior has been observed again and again in Deaf communities around the world: in the USA,[40] France,[41] Japan,[42] and China.[43] Why? How can it be explained? Simply because when someone looks you straight in the eyes, you don't need to hear your name to know that that person is talking to you, not to someone else. The use of names is necessary only when we talk to people without looking at them, or look at them perfunctorily, or for a split second. If you are not convinced, try the following experiment:

In a meeting of your choice, look someone straight in the eyes, and ask a question starting with the name of the person sitting next to him or her. Then, enjoy the confusion. The confusion of the person you are looking at, that of the person to whom you addressed the question, and that of the people watching the interaction.

Once you have tested the efficiency of Deaf eye contact, you won't go back to your Hearing habits. Today, I can no longer talk to people who are reading a document, playing with their cell phone, or looking at their computer. When it happens, just like my Deaf colleagues, I stop talking until I get their attention again, and then, with a big smile, I say: "I need to see your eyes to better understand you."

Read my lips

The eyes are the first place where we should look for information. The lips should come right after. We – Hearing people as much as Deaf people – have been reading lips since we were very young, without even being aware of it. We look at people's lips as soon as the ambient noise rises. We stare at lips when the other person has a slight accent. We read lips when we are separated by a window, to say *good bye*. We read lips in meetings to try to get what people are saying in side conversations. We read lips to communicate behind the teacher's or the manager's back. We read lips to sing in church when there are no more hymn books available.[44] We read lips during social events, or at friends' when our partner is tired or bored, and wants to leave. We read lips to shorten the visit of an apartment we don't like, to avoid hurting the feelings of the owner. We read lips all the time, even if we have not sharpened this skill as much as we could have.

Bonnie: After my studies, I worked at a hospital specialized in spinal cord injuries. It was a difficult job. Most of the people who were sent there were paralyzed from head to toe. One morning, I entered the room of a new patient, smiled at him, and asked him if he had slept well. It was a routine question. He smiled back at me. I checked all the monitoring systems and then asked if he was comfortable. The man smiled at me again and said: "Very comfortable, thank you. I don't feel a thing."
Bruno: Incredible! That man was completely paralyzed and he was making fun of it?
Bonnie: Indeed. I laughed at his joke, but as I did, he started to cry.
Bruno: Why?
Bonnie: At first, I thought that I had hurt him with my laugh. So I quickly apologized. But when I did, he said: "Please don't apologize... Are you real?" It was a strange question. I thought that he was still in shock and was rambling. But then he went on: "Can you really understand me? Are you able to read my lips?"
Bruno: Oh. I get it. His vocal cords were not working anymore? He could not produce any sound?

Bonnie: That's right. Because of the tracheotomy and the respiratory tubes, his lips were still moving, but he was unable to talk. He had tried to interact with other nurses and doctors, but no one could understand him.
Bruno: That's terrible!
Bonnie: Yes. I wiped the tears from his face – while retaining my own – and started to answer all the questions he had about his new situation.[45]

First the eyes, then the lips. And once you are comfortable with both, then look at the rest of the body to have a final confirmation that what you have captured and interpreted is right.

The rest of the body

Emmanuelle: When I was a child one of my favorite games was to observe people.
Bruno: To observe people?
Emmanuelle: Yes. To look at their body talk. I would look at the way they walked, the way they sat, the way they talked. I would look at the way they looked or didn't look at others while talking. At the way they nervously played with an object close at hand: a pen or a fork, or with part of their body: their hair, their hands or fingers.
Bruno: And?
Emmanuelle: And by observing their body movements I was able to tell without any error if they were angry, irritated, happy, sad, or surprised, I was even able to tell what type of relationship they had with the people they were interacting with.[46]

Unconsciously, we all read body language. If this wasn't the case, we would systematically bump into one another when walking on a crowded sidewalk, and we would not be able to shake hands or to play ball. Without reading body language, we would not feel sad when someone cries, or joyful when someone laughs. If we were not able to read body language, we could not fall in love. We all read body language... but maybe not as much as we should. Do we always notice when we talk when people are tired, when they have something to say, when they are uncomfortable with what we say, or when they don't have a clue as to what we are talking about? Are we able to read other people's body language like Deaf people do?

David: Like, for example, seeing when someone reaches the end of a conversation on the phone.
Bruno: How would you know something like that?

David: By the micro movements of the hand on the receiver, a slight shift of the body posture, a quick change of the facial expression showing that the person talking has just decided to move on to something else. Minute but sure signs which only the eyes can capture.

Bruno: So Hearing people could also see those clues if they paid more attention?

David: Yes. I think so. If they indeed wanted to. They could even push it further, guessing with whom the person is talking to on the phone. I'm able to do it with the people I know well, just by looking at their facial expression and body stance. We all have different subpersonalities living in us. And depending on who we are talking to, we activate one or another of them.

Bruno: I have noticed this phenomenon with my wife and with a colleague of mine. Their voices completely change depending on who is on the other end of the phone. But I've never seen any physical change...

David: Because you don't pay enough attention. Most of the time Hearing people don't see those changes. Maybe because they believe they don't need to see them. They trust sound so much - maybe too much. Deaf people see them because they have no other choice. It's the only source of information they have access to. And since people often say things they don't believe, and contrary to words, our bodies never lie, so Deaf people – who are frequently seen as disabled – are in fact often in the paradoxical situation of seeing what they are not supposed to: the true thoughts and feelings of people...[47]

When we interact with people, we can choose to remain at the level of their words, and believe what they say, or we can move on to nonverbal communication, and understand and believe what their body says. The first choice is quick and easy, the second requires some courage and effort. The first choice comforts us in the belief that everything is for the best in the best of all worlds, while the second forces us to clarify feelings and to face potential issues. The first creates a social, courteous rapport, the second a trustful, intimate relationship.

When you ask to someone "How are you?" and when the answer is "Fine," do you stop there? Are you satisfied with the answer, or do you dare to read their body language which might scream: "I've better things to do than be here with you. I was forced to come here, so I'll be polite and I'll stay, but don't ask for more than that. Now, let's get this over with." If words give you access to what people say, you can tell what they really feel and think by the contraction of their muscles and their change in skin color.

On a trip to Bangkok, the cabin crew told me about a passenger on a previous flight who had refused everything that had been offered: cocktails, snacks, lunch, and dinner. When he arrived at destination and was told by a friend that all this was complimentary, he got mad and wrote a letter to the airline complaining about the quality of the service he had received on board. As I reflected on this anecdote, I couldn't refrain from wondering whose fault it was: the man for not having the humility and courage to ask, or the cabin crew's for not having been able to read the body language of someone who was flying for the first time.

If you want to be more successful in life, if you want to have a more profound relationship with someone, adopt the Deaf way: give your ears a break, listen with your eyes.

Deaf Tip n°2: Read body language
Exercises

- Teaching others is the best way to learn. Share something you have learned in this chapter with at least three friends, colleagues, or members of your family.
- Think about the three people you selected in the introduction. Do you know the color of their eyes? How would you move your body if you were to imitate them? What is the specific tick of each of them? Don't move on to the next chapter before you know.
- How long can you maintain eye contact? Count in your head, during your next interaction with someone. Then, try to make your eye contact last longer in the following interactions.
- Watch a movie you have never seen before with a friend. Turn the sound off. Guess what the actors say by observing their body language. Have a quick chat with your friend to compare your ideas, and then turn the sound on to check who was right.
- Try to have a full conversation with the person you love the most without making a sound, only by reading lips.
- Observe people in a restaurant or in a park. How do they walk? How do they sit? How are they dressed? What is their personality? What is their relationship? What are they talking about? How do they get along? Do they have children? What is their level of education? In what field? What type of job do they have? What type of car do they drive? Try to describe their house or their apartment. Do this exercise with a friend, and then compare your thoughts.
- When you go to work tomorrow, don't say *Hello* to people, say *How are you this morning?* and then listen with your eyes.
- Remember the Deaf rule: If one cannot see, one cannot hear. For a full week, whenever possible, avoid e-mail, phone calls, sms, or shouting. Get out of your chair, and go talk to people *face-to-face*. At the end of the week, try to evaluate if it helped improve your relationships with others.
- What could you do to improve your communication with the three people you selected in the introduction?
- Practice, practice, practice.
- Once done, move on to another chapter.

Personal Notes

· ·

· ·

· ·

· ·

· ·

· ·

· ·

· ·

· ·

· ·

· ·

· ·

· ·

Only that in you which is me
can hear what I'm saying
Richard Alpert, American Professor of Psychology

Deaf Tip n°3
Put yourself in the other's shoes

Why is it impossible to find mouse, bird, or fly flavored food[48] in pet food stores? Why can we only find beef, lamb, and chicken cans knowing that no cat has ever caught any of those animals to eat them? Simply because we all believe that everybody – our family, our friends, our neighbors… and even our pets – see the world as we do, and have the same *good* taste as we have. And whenever we try to look at the world through the eyes of someone else we are so unused to it that we inevitably commit gaffes.

Vicky: One day, as I was boarding a plane, a member of the cabin crew greeted me with a warm hello. I replied by signing hello in French Sign Language.[49]
Bruno: To show that you're Deaf, I guess. Did she understand?
Vicky: Yes. She smiled, looked at my boarding card, and guided me to my seat. While people were boarding, I saw that she kept on looking at me.
Bruno: Why?
Vicky: No idea. Then, when all the passengers were seated, she started to explain the pre-flight safety demonstration: how to buckle the seatbelt, how to place the oxygen mask in case of depressurization, etc. And in between two explanations, she was bending over me, saying: I will show you after.
Bruno: Show you what?
Vicky: I don't know. I travel by plane every weekend. I had seen this safety demonstration so many times that I could have done it myself. At the end of the presentation, she showed the passengers that there was a safety card in the back of the seat in front of them, and told me discreetly that she would give me one later.
Bruno: You didn't have one in front of you?
Vicky: I had one. So I was puzzled. As the aircraft was ready to take off, she came back to me, and said: "You know, for security reasons, you also need to get familiar with the safety instructions," and she gave me a safety card written in Braille.
Bruno: In Braille?!

Vicky: Yes, in Braille! I was mad. I told her that I wasn't blind, I was Deaf. I saw in her eyes that it suddenly clicked. She didn't know what to do. She apologized over and over, sat down, and buckled up.

We are all locked in our own little worlds, thinking that everybody is like us. The first time I became conscious of this was during my military service. I was 18. On the first day, the sergeant gave us a pack which included underwear and a toiletries kit. The tightie-whities were big enough to be used as parachutes, the toothpaste strong enough to unblock the toilet, and the razors big enough to be used as close combat knives. We all laughed about it and threw them away. Then, I saw a young man who not only kept his, but, despite the sarcastic comments of the other guys, went to the garbage to recover those we had thrown away. We were all complaining about every single aspect of life in the army, but he was telling us how great everything was. We were criticizing the food, he was eating it. We were counting the hours before the weekend to go home, he was staying there because he had no other place to go. The army had become his family, his home. There, he had a bed, food, clothes, and even a certain form of love. In 18 years, growing up in an opulent country, I had never met or even thought that someone just a few miles away from my home could be cold or hungry. I had always thought that poor people lived in faraway lands. This happened to me 30 years ago and it was such a shock, that I still have the face of this young man engraved in my mind.

Empathy is the ability to relate to others by putting ourselves in their shoes, to feel the emotions they are experiencing. But how can we do this if we have never felt the same emotions?

Carlo: Most of my friends have Hearing parents who didn't learn to sign.
Bruno: How do they communicate then?
Carlo: They don't… As a child, one of them, signed to his mom: "Mom, I love you."
Bruno: And?
Carlo: And his mother slapped his hands. She didn't want him to sign. She wanted him to talk. She wanted her son to be like her.
Bruno: That's terrible!
Carlo: To this day, when my friend tells this story, he's still very emotional.

Because they have been *there*, Deaf people are often more attentive and sensitive to other people's needs, which of course tremendously improves their communication. Could we do the same? Could we focus less on ourselves, and more on the people around us? If this is what you want, a good way to start is by asking yourselves the six following Deaf questions:

Can you see from someone else's perspective?

Emmanuelle: When I was a child one day my mother took me to visit one of her friends. As they were talking over a cup of tea, I felt I needed to go to the toilet, but I didn't want to bother them. Usually I asked my mother to come with me, but that day, I decided to manage by myself.

Bruno: How old were you?

Emmanuelle: Less than six. I found the bathroom and locked the door behind me as I had seen adults do. But a few minutes later when I tried to reopen the door, I couldn't. The lock was stuck. I tried again and again but couldn't. I started to panic. So, I began to scream, but no one seemed to hear me. So I banged as hard as I could on the door. I was so terrified.

Bruno: And your mother?

Emmanuelle: She was of course behind the door, trying to reassure me. But how could I know? How could I hear her comforting words? The door was blocking our communication. I couldn't hear her since I couldn't see her.

Bruno: Scary!

Emmanuelle: Yes. Then, I saw a piece of paper slide under the door. As I didn't know yet how to read, my mom had drawn a comic strip: a child crying with a big cross over and next to it the same child with a big smile. She was asking me to stop crying. But there was nothing about the door. So I thought that she was telling me that I would have to spend the rest of my life in that bathroom forced to smile. As a result I panicked even more, screamed even louder, and banged even harder on the door until a locksmith came and saved me.[50]

We constantly reduce everything to our own experience, thinking that our logic is the same as everyone else's logic, that our thoughts are the same as everyone else's thoughts. That is how we are. And if you think you are different, then play this little game with your friends or your family. Talk for five minutes about a topic of your choice without using the words *I*, *me*, *myself*, *my*, or *mine*. You will be surprised to find how difficult it is. And this is precisely where the problem lies. In order to relate to others we need to shift our focus from what *we* need and want, to what *they* need and want. And to achieve this, we must feel *with* them (empathy), not *for* them (sympathy). It is not because I want my daughter to stop crying that she wants to as well. If I try to stop being me for a while, and really put myself in another's shoes, feeling for a few seconds what a six year old little girl locked in a room might feel, I will quickly understand that the problem is not the tears but the door.

Do you adapt your language to others?

To improve communication, Deaf people constantly adapt their language to the people they are talking to, switching from Sign Language,[51] to iconicity,[52] or to mime.[53] Depending if they are interacting with other Deaf people who share the same Sign Language, Deaf people who use a different Sign Language,[54] Deaf oralists who are not fluent in Sign Language, Hearing people who know Sign Language, Hearing people who know a few signs, or Hearing people who know no signs at all, they will choose either rapid and complex Sign Language, slow and simple Sign language, iconicity, or mime, always checking that the other person understands.

When, for example, a Deaf French signer wishes to say to another Deaf French signer "Let's walk" she or he will express it in Sign Language with the hand closed, facing down, the index and the middle finger in a hook shape, moving away from the body. If the interlocutor is not fluent in Sign Language, the Deaf person will turn to iconicity, using the middle finger as the right leg, the index as the left, making them walk like a human being in a specific direction. If the other still does not understand, the Deaf person will then have recourse to mime, using the whole body to mimic, like the mime, Marcel Marceau, the walking action. What about you? Do you adapt your language to the age, education, and culture of the people you are talking to, or do you expect them to make an effort?

Years ago, I was part of a European delegation working in Russia with fifty top local executives and government representatives to launch a new project. A German colleague who was sitting next to me had just finished a very complex explanation, when one of the CEOs, sitting on the opposite side of the huge table, said with a strong accent: "Excuse me Sir, I don't understand. Can you please repeat?" We were all shocked by the answer of our colleague: "I will not repeat, for if I did, I would use the exact same words." Quickly, other colleagues took over and reformulated what had been said in a different way, saving the project. Once the meeting was over, I went to see that colleague to understand why he had been so rude. As we were discussing what had happened, I was surprised to discover that his behavior was not so much due to the fact that he didn't want to reformulate as his inability to do so.

Unfortunately, this anecdote is not one of a kind. More often than we think, we all get stuck in our own limited lingo, having a hard time saying the same thing in a different way. Last month, I was with my spouse in Beijing. As we were talking at a table in a restaurant, the waitress came over and asked if we were ready to order. "Can you give us two minutes?" Magali asked politely. The waitress left and came back a few minutes later with two dishes which I guess for her sounded like the word *minutes*. Surprised, Magali tried to correct the situation. "I asked for two *minutes*," she said "I didn't ask for these two dishes" [Blank look on the face of the waitress]. So, she tried again: "OK, can you please give us five minutes?" I burst out laughing, visualizing what would happen. "Honey, she will come back with five of the same dish!" I tried a different approach. I raised my hand in the international sign meaning stop, don't move, and said in an authoritative tone: "Wait." The waitress stopped, and waited for us to order.

We must adapt our language to the people we interact with even if we also need to acknowledge that adaptability has its limits. One day, Jean-Philippe, a colleague of mine, received an e-mail from a client who called him Jean-Pierre. All the people who were in copy to this e-mail were curious to see how he would react. How would he correct the client without making him feel uncomfortable? We were all surprised to read his reply. In his e-mail there wasn't a single allusion to the client's mistake. On the contrary, he ended his e-mail by signing: *Best regards, Jean-Pierre*. The problem, however, with such adaptability, is that today everybody, the client, as well as his colleagues, call him Jean-Pierre!

Do you exclude others with your words?

Anyone who has ever talked to an IT specialist, and who has survived the experience, knows what it feels like to be excluded. Here is an extract from an interaction with a hot line:

"Hello."
"Hello. What can I do to help you?"
"I just bought a modem to go online and play with my Xbox at the same time. I followed the instructions on the CD Rom, but it doesn't work."
"Of course. You need to go to your Local Area Connection."
"The Local Area Connection?"
"Highlight the internet protocol TCP/IP."
"The proto-what?"
"Then close the LAN properties. Disable and enable back your Local Area Connection. Now, check your NIC. If it doesn't work, reinstall its driver."
[sobbing]
"Or you can access your router using IE8, http//192.168.2.1 to change your Connection Type into PPPoA instead of PPPoE. See, it's easy."
[Gunshot]

This type of language does not only occur in technical environments. Every group – professional and social – quickly develops a specific language, a kind of secret code, to strengthen the bond between its members. A bond which gets stronger every time someone who does not understand this language gets rejected… even if that person is a customer!

A friend of mine who is a member of an airline cabin crew enjoys telling the story of an old lady who was flying for the first time. A flight attendant who had been doing the job for too long, took her boarding pass, and said "You're sitting on the wing" which in airline jargon means "Your seat is at the level of the wings." Hearing that, the old lady turned white, and in a shaky voice replied "I would prefer to sit inside the plane, please."

If technical language is dysfunctional for neophytes, acronyms are dysfunctional for everybody. Acronyms are non-human. Have you ever heard a child use acronyms? No. Only adults do. What is a DMC? Is it a:

- Data Management Coordinator
- Domestic Management Code
- Development Milestone Chart
- Direct Maintenance Cost
- Distributed Master Control
- Data Module Code, or
- Digital Media Catalog?[55]

Not so long ago I witnessed an argument between a manager and one of his team members. Both were arguing in front of the team about PDP. They quickly became frustrated with each other, and their tone of voice started to rise. I could see that the people present in the room didn't understand what was going on. After a while, the manager finally asked:

"What do you mean by PDP?"
"I'm talking about my Personal Development Plan … Aren't you?"
"Of course not! I would not do that in front of everybody! I was talking about all the problems we currently have on the Product Development Program, and I was wondering why you were bringing everything back to you all the time!"

Technical language and acronyms are a plague. And contrary to what people think, they were not invented to be precise or to gain time, but to give to a minority of people a feeling of power over a majority, which of course can only create feelings of frustration, rejection, and put an end to any form of empathy, and consequently to good communication.

Do you place words in the right order?

In most Hearing languages, when you want to place the focus on a word, you simply position it at the beginning of a sentence. "Yesterday I read a book" does not have the same meaning as "I read a book yesterday" or "the book I read yesterday…" The first syntax emphasizes *when* I read the book, the second *who* reads the book, and the last *what* I read. In theory, a sentence can start with any of its parts – noun, verb, adjective – depending on what we wish to emphasize. But in reality, most Hearing people's sentences start with the subject, the most common one being *I*. I am the protagonist of my speech. I am the center of the world. Compared to Deaf practices, this is shocking. Here is a concrete example. While Hearing people would say "I put the TV on the table" unconsciously revealing their egocentric vision of the world, and their desperate need to exist, Deaf people sign "On the table the TV I place." The objective of such syntax is not to be as cool as Yoda, but to avoid breaking the TV. If you have a heavy TV in your arms, but no table to put it on, you are in trouble. If, on the other hand, you first describe a table, and then enter the room with a heavy TV, even if it is only in words, you will be happy to have a place to safely put it. So logical! Just like with a painting, a play, or a book, to help the other visualize and consequently better understand our message we must describe first the environment, then the characters, and only at the end, the action.

According to research done by Goldin-Meadow, whatever the culture or language, speakers who are forced to use gestures or pictures instead of sound to express themselves, automatically give up the usual subject-verb-object order, and place the verb, and consequently the subject, at the end of the sentence, like in Sign Language, as if this order – placing ourselves after others – was more natural.[56] This linguistic research supports what we experience on a daily basis. Focusing too much on ourselves can only lead to sorrow. By carefully selecting the order of our words, we show respect to others which is refreshing in a world where self-centeredness has become the norm. What do you usually say? "Me and my friends are…" or "my friends and I are…" Which is the most appropriate, the most polite? In the first case, you inform people that you are more important than your friends. In the second, you show humility and respect. Do you say: "My wife Sandra…" or "Sandra, my wife…"? In the first case, you place the focus on her role, in the second on her as an individual. In the first case, you express – even if unconsciously – that you see her as one of your many belongings. In the second, that she is your life partner.

Do you make other people's life easy?

Once the words are right, and in the right order, then you are all set to put yourself in the other person's shoes. Deaf people always go out of their way to make it easy for others to understand. For example, when you ask directions from a Deaf person, they will physically move and stand next to you, shoulder to shoulder, in order to allow you to follow their directions without any effort: "Go straight, turn right, turn left" (indicating straight, right, and left). Hearing people will tend to give you directions facing you, also using their hands, saying right and showing their right – which is your left – forcing you to invert every single detail of the directions in your mind. I once saw a Deaf friend giving directions to a Hearing person while facing her. I was surprised to see that in this case, he stayed in front of her, but inverted all the signs: "Go straight" (his thumb indicating a straight line towards his back), "Turn right" (showing with his index finger his left), "and then take the second road on the left" (showing his right), doing whatever was necessary to make the woman's life as easy as possible.

How can we apply this principle to our daily lives? A good place to start is with the way we write e-mail. Do you regularly receive e-mails as long as a book with an endless list of attachments as if people were throwing out all their frustrations, worries or ideas at you? Once done, they might indeed feel relief, but what about the people who receive this type of e-mail? What did they need? And what did they receive? Maybe they just wanted one word or one slide. There is only one way to write a good e-mail: it is by putting ourselves in the other person's shoes, asking ourselves what the other person wants, and limiting ourselves to answering only that question.

Do you postpone your judgment?

The final Deaf question we should ask ourselves to be more sensitive to other people's needs is related to judgment. We all judge all the time. Is it going to be hot, cold, or rainy today? Just with a quick look out the window we judge the weather, and decide what we will wear for the day. When going to work and the cars in front of us suddenly slow down, we quickly judge again. How severe is the situation? How long will it last? It takes us just a few seconds to decide if we should slow down and wait, or take another route. We need to evaluate our environment constantly. And we do it by judging. If we didn't, we would not be able to make a single decision. But judging events is not as complex and delicate as judging people. If I judge that I should wear a shirt instead of a sweater, the worst thing that can happen is that I catch cold. It is not quite the same when I have to judge someone who killed someone else, knowing that my judgment will have a lifelong effect on the defendant, on the relatives of the person who died, and on society. Is the accused a murderer who should be punished, a psychopath who should be treated, a victim who should be acquitted, or a hero who should be rewarded?[57] Hopefully, we will never have to pronounce such judgments, but on a less dramatic level, we constantly do it in the office, in the street, and in our own homes, often putting an end to a relationship or communication before it has even started.

Regularly, at the beginning of my communication courses, my Deaf colleagues sit in the training room, reading or writing messages on their cell phones, waiting for the training course to start. As trainees arrive, I greet them at the door and invite them to take a seat. They enter the room and often say hello to the Deaf trainers who do not reply as they are looking at their phones and cannot hear the greeting. I observe the body language of those trainees which most of the time visibly expresses discontent. I can read on their faces: "How rude! I said hello, and they didn't reply. They even didn't look at me!" Then, the course starts. While I am doing the introduction, my Deaf colleagues, who are sitting in the back, act as if they are listening to what I say. And I see the irritated trainees regularly glancing at them with cross looks. Then, we do a round table and my Deaf colleagues introduce themselves in Sign Language. I observe the frustrated trainees with a smile and see when it suddenly clicks. All their muscles relax and a smile appears. They understand that they were not impolite, that they just couldn't hear their greetings, and consequently couldn't answer. During the break I often go and talk with those people, and I am somewhat amused to hear them say that they first felt irritation, anger, and resentment, and then embarrassment, guilt, and regret when they understood that they had misjudged people.

This can also happen in our daily lives. And we don't require Deaf people around us to misjudge. Not so long ago, at the end of a lunch I had in one of the Airbus restaurants, as I was walking out, I saw one of my former trainees, a top manager, eating alone. I walked over to him and said hello. He looked at me, but didn't reply. Just as if I wasn't there. No emotion on his face, no message in his eyes. I walked away feeling very uncomfortable. What was wrong? Why did he look at me that way? For several days, it haunted me. I asked one of my colleagues who was working at the time with his team if he had any idea what the problem could be. He didn't know. Two or three weeks later I came across this manager again. We both had to take the same elevator. After a few polite words about family and business, feeling that our relationship was as good as before, I asked:

"Pierre, a few weeks ago, you were eating alone in the restaurant. I said hello, but you didn't reply. Is there anything wrong between us?"
"Wrong? Of course not. Why do you say that?"
"Well, because I was standing in front of you, and you looked at me without any reaction!"
"Bruno, nothing was wrong, except maybe that I'm overworked. I must have been lost in my thoughts. I'm sorry."

Well, what is wrong with this story is not so much that that manager was lost in his thoughts, than my rush to judge, and my lack of courage to sit down at that very moment and clarify the situation with him. If we don't want to feel irritation, anger, resentment, embarrassment, guilt, or regret, then we need to postpone judgment, because we might be wrong, and because, one day, we might be in the same situation as the person we are judging.

Madan: I was born in India, in a loving family, and have very fond memories of my childhood. Then, at the age of twelve, my life felt apart. I caught the mumps and had typhoid fever for two weeks. My fever was so high that I was unconscious for several days. The next thing I remember is waking up one morning completely deaf.
Bruno: How did you react to that?
Madan: I was terrified. The only deaf person I knew was an old man in our village who was mentally retarded. People always made fun of him because he looked more like an animal than a human being: his body was deformed, he growled like a dog, and as no one took care of him, he hadn't washed or changed clothes for years. And I'm ashamed to say that I was like everybody else... My friends and I loved to tease him until he got mad and made all sorts of scary noises. We would then run away laughing.
Bruno: So what happened when you became deaf?
Madan: I suddenly realized that now, I was like that old man. I was lying in my bed seeing myself old, deformed, wearing torn clothes, and growling at people who made fun of me. I would then hide my head under the blanket and cry silently at this awful vision of my future.[58]

Every human being is a room with a locked door. And we naively believe that the key to our own door fits the locks of other doors. But it doesn't work that way. Each door has a unique lock, and if we want to open the door to someone else, we must forge a new key which fits their lock.[59] And the only way to find the shape of the key is by carefully listening to them, putting ourselves in their shoes, looking through their eyes, and without any judgment, adapting our language and our behavior to them.

Deaf Tip n°3: Put yourself in the other's shoes
Exercises

- Teaching others is the best way to learn. Share something you have learned in this chapter with at least three friends, colleagues, or members of your family.
- Observe yourself for a week. Do you adapt your language to people? Pay attention to the way they talk, the words they use, their flow of words, their accent and intonation. How close can you get to their talking style without being noticed?
- What are the three acronyms you use the most? What do they mean? Get rid of them, and from now own use more appropriate wording.
- With your index finger, write the letter Q on your forehead. Did you write it for you or for someone who would be reading it? Next time you explain something to someone sitting on the other side of a table, write or draw upside down, and see how easy/difficult it is, and how people react to it.
- Think about someone you don't like. What is his/her major strength, or skill?
- Ask a friend or a colleague to listen to you for five minutes. How many times did you use the words *I*, *me*, *myself*, *my*, or *mine*? Next time, reduce the number.
- For an entire day, don't write e-mail to only say what you have on your mind. Think about what people need or want, and delete the rest.
- Think about one of the three people you selected in the introduction. Say: my name is (say the name of that person). Describe yourself as if you were that person: your height, color of hair, your job, the type of relationship you have with people. Use *I*, not *he* or *she*. Then, slowly, move to your relationship. What do you think, feel, or need (being he or she)? Don't impose your own thoughts. Talk as if you were that person, and observe how you feel, and what your thoughts are.
- Borrow a few CDs from your friends of artists you have never heard before. Listen to all the tracks, and try to understand why your friends like them.
- Invest a few hours a week in a volunteer group to support your local school, visit people in prison, guide job seekers, feed the homeless, help the abused, etc.
- What can you do to improve your communication with the three people you selected in the introduction?
- Practice, practice, practice.
- Once done, move on to another chapter.

Personal Notes

The shortest way to do many things
is to do only one thing at a time.
Sir Richard Cecil, English Politician

Deaf Tip n°4
Be sequential

In one of my initial meetings with Deaf people, I used an interpreter – which in itself was a strange situation: looking at one person while listening to another. During the conversation, I was struck by something which was said, so I started to write it down in my notebook. Suddenly the atmosphere changed. I looked up and saw the young woman I was talking to frowning angrily at me.

Bruno: What's wrong?
Morgane: You're being very rude!
Bruno: Rude? Why?
Morgane: Because you just interrupted the conversation.
Bruno: What do you mean, I interrupted the conversation? I haven't stopped listening to you, even when I was writing!
Morgane: When you stopped looking at me, you put an end to the communication between us.
Bruno: I'm sorry, but what you said was so interesting that I didn't want to forget it. That's why I was writing.
Morgane: No, Bruno. You don't write something down because you are afraid of forgetting it. You forget when you write! [It took me a while to understand this new concept]
Bruno: Come on! What are you saying? That because you aren't taking notes, you are able to remember everything we are saying?
Morgane: Yes. I do only one thing at a time. And since I don't write, I'm more present in the interaction. Consequently, I can concentrate more on our exchange. And the more I concentrate, the more I remember.

Ten days later, when I met her again, she was able to recall not just everything we had said during our meeting, but also the color of my shirt, the color of my tie, and even how many chairs there had been in the room. Without knowing it, Deaf people strictly apply the famous Buddhist principle exemplified in the following tale:

Amazed by all the tasks his Zen master could accomplish in one day, the apprentice asked him to share his secret. The master replied: "When I sit, I sit. When I stand, I stand. And when I walk, I walk." The disciple said that he was doing the same, but still couldn't achieve as much in a day. "No," replied the master, "You don't do the same. When you sit, you already stand up. When you stand, you already walk. And when you walk, you have already arrived."

When Deaf people communicate, they communicate. They avoid doing anything else at the same time. Unlike Hearing people, they don't watch TV, surf the internet, play with their smartphone, or watch people walk by when they interact with someone. It is just not part of their culture. In a recent meeting I had with a group of Deaf facilitators, I presented to them a new way of working together. I gave each of them a paper copy with a detailed description of it, and started to elaborate on it as they were reading the material. After a few seconds, one of them stopped me and asked if they should first read the document, and then we could discuss it, or if we should discuss it first, and then they would read the document. Focusing on both tasks at the same time was difficult for them – but not impossible – their eyes being either on the document, or on the interpreter. In contrast, because their eyes and ears are working, Hearing people believe that they can do two things at the same time, which of course is self-deception. Nobody can. Neither Deaf people, nor Hearing people.

One at a time to better understand

Gina: When I was in 6th grade, there was a group of girls I wanted so much to hang around with. They were cool. They were pretty. They were funny. But most of all, they always looked like they were having so much fun together. This is one of the worst memories I have from my school years.
Bruno: Why? Did they reject you?
Gina: No. Not at all. Or at least not consciously. They would simply sit together in the cafeteria or on the stairs of the school and talk, talk, talk. But I couldn't capture one single word.
Bruno: Why? You're not completely deaf, and you can read lips, can't you?
Gina: Yes. Except when people talk at the same time. When they do, the only thing I hear is a rumbling noise. And as I can only look at one mouth at the time, the time it takes me to understand that the person has stopped talking and find the next pair of moving lips, a third, fourth, or even fifth person has already spoken. In this case, it's impossible to follow a conversation. So I was sitting there, on the side, by myself, sad and frustrated.[60]

It is impossible for Deaf people to listen to several people talking at the same time, just as it is impossible for Hearing people. It is impossible to listen to two people talking at the same time. It is impossible to listen to someone and to yourself talking at the same time, and it is impossible to have two simultaneous dialogues or even two thoughts at the same time. Try it. Select two different topics and try to think about them at the same time. It is impossible. The closest you can get is constantly switching from one topic to the other, even if it is just for a few seconds.

Then why, when people are talking, do we try to guess their next words, instead of letting them finish and listening carefully to what they have to say? Maybe because we love the sound of our own voice so much. Maybe because we are convinced that what we have to say is more interesting, or closer to the truth? Maybe because when we talk, we feel so much more alive. Or maybe simply because when we all talk at the same time we feel that we can squeeze more information into the same time frame.

If you have ever lived abroad, you have surely noticed that the time people are allotted to talk greatly varies according to the culture. While in Germany people tend to guess the last word of your sentences; in France, people quickly get impatient and have the feeling that you are being way too slow to get to the point, so in the middle of your sentences, they will finish them for you, even if they have no idea what you want to say. And of course, the farther south you go, the worst it gets. In Spain and in Italy, as soon as you start talking everybody else starts talking at the same time!

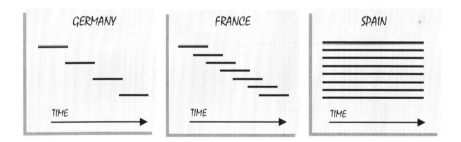

This is a growing tendency. Even Google does it now. When you search for something on the internet, as soon as you start typing a word, Google tries to finish for you. You want to go on vacation, so to get some ideas, you open Google, and start typing the two first letters: V… A… As soon as you have done so, Google finishes the word for you, suggesting VAns, VAnity fairs, or VAmpire diaries. Can I please finish my word?

This would rarely happen in the Deaf world. To focus on the interaction, Deaf people always follow a strict protocol: only one person signs at a time while the others observe. And if a person interrupts, all the people involved in the conversation shake their right hand, their arm placed horizontally, to signify to the disturber that he or she must wait until the person who is signing has finished. But that is not all. Not only do Deaf people wait for others to finish what they have to say, but they also leave a visual blank between two interactions, in order to be sure that the person who is signing is really done. Their communication can be represented as follows:

This approach presents many advantages. First, as everyone focuses on the signer, respect quickly rises in the group, encouraging people to express themselves more freely. Second, by being sequential, Deaf people make sure that they first understand the other person before trying to be understood,[61] in this way avoiding many misunderstandings. Finally, despite the fact that for new comers this protocol might seem at first a bit slow, an agreement is always reached faster than during a typical overlapping Hearing discussion.[62]

Resolve conflicts one at a time

It is difficult, of course, to remain silent and sequential when emotions are strong. I was called one day as a mediator to help a team resolve an internal conflict in which they were stuck. The manager had previously briefed me on the problem. In every meeting two of his senior team members were systematically confrontational, raising the tone of their voices after only a few minutes. I asked him if I could observe his team before making any recommendations. He agreed. When I observed them during their next team meeting, everything happened exactly as he had described. After only five minutes, the two team members were red-faced, nearly screaming at each other, while the rest of the team remained silent, looking at their shoes. The manager asked them to calm down several times, without succeeding. Not knowing what to do, he finally left the room, and the two men kept on arguing, blaming and accusing one another, not even noticing that everyone had left. The following week, before the meeting started, I placed a stress ball on the table and said: "From now on, nobody in this room is allowed to talk without holding this power toy. And no one can say anything without first repeating what the previous person has said."[63] As soon as I had finished my sentence, one of the two guys quickly grabbed the ball and started to complain about the other. Everyone could feel that he was trying to raise his voice, but as there was no opposition to fuel his anger – I was carefully controlling the other guy with all the body language I could use – escalation was impossible. He finally finished his litany with a hesitant "… and that's all I wanted to say." He replaced the stress ball on the table, and the other quickly grabbed it, and started to attack his colleague, but I stopped him immediately, asking him, as agreed at the start of the meeting, to first reformulate what his colleague had said. He was unable to. So I gave the stress ball back to the first team member, and asked him to repeat what he had said, which he did in a much less emotional way. He then replaced the toy on the table. The other team member took it, and repeated carefully what his colleague had said. He went on with his own complaints, trying also to raise his voice, but to no avail as there was no opposition expressed. As a consequence, he rapidly calmed down, and simply said what he had to say.

For about a full year these two guys had been stuck in an aggressive mode of communication, talking at the same time, not listening to one another, throwing negative emotions in each other's faces and at the whole team. And by simply using a toy, forcing them to talk in a sequential manner, and consequently forcing them to really listen to each other, within only two meetings these two men were able to communicate once again in a sensible manner. I saw the manager a few months later, and questioned him about his team. He told me that the two men were still behaving correctly, and whenever he felt that things were slipping again, he would swiftly improvise a power toy with his smart phone, a bottle, or a pen and good habits would quickly return.

This approach of sequential communication works as effectively in the corporate world as in our private lives. It just needs a little adaptation. Some years ago, I was tired of coming home every night and finding my children fighting with one another without ever reaching a happy end. It seemed to me that this was occurring every day. And it didn't fit with my vision of what a family should be. After much reading, a lot of observation of Deaf conflict resolution, and some pondering, I came back home one day with a table, three chairs and a scrap book, and I called for a special family meeting to present my plan:

"This table is the Dialogue Table" I said solemnly. "This table is strictly reserved for resolving conflicts between members of our family. No one is allowed to sit at this table at any other time, for any other reason. Whenever you feel slighted by a member of the family, you have the right to ask for the Dialogue Table. And when you are requested to sit at the Dialogue Table by someone who has been slighted, you are required to sit at the table. The two people in conflict will sit in two of the chairs, while a mediator, appointed because he or she has no part in the conflict, will sit in the third chair. The role of the mediator is to make sure that the people sitting at the Dialogue Table respect the rules. Do we all agree to sit at the Dialogue Table when asked by someone and to leave it only when negative feelings have completely disappeared?"

As the whole family was curious to see how this table and chairs would resolve our problems, they all voted yes. I then placed on the Dialogue Table the scrap book, and read the rules which were written on the first page:

(1) You must come to the Dialogue Table whenever a member of our family asks you to.
(2) The Mediator can never give his point of view or take the side of one person.
(3) The Mediator reminds the people in conflict of the rules of the Dialogue Table (points 4 to 11).
(4) Both the offender and the offended person agree to respect the Mediator's decisions and facilitation.
(5) The person who feels offended, and asked for the Dialogue Table, starts. The sentences of the person offended must start with the words "I," for example: "I felt…" "I heard…" "I understood…" etc., not with the word "you."
(6) The offender listens without interrupting.
(7) Once the offended person is done, the offender slowly and silently counts until three, and then reformulates what the offended person has said. If the offender is not able to reformulate, or if the reformulation is not accurate, the process starts all over again at rule 5.
(8) When the reformulation is correct, the offended person confirms with a sign of the head, without talking, or adding anything.
(9) The offender can then give his or her point of view. Sentences must once again avoid the accusing "you" and use "I" to express personal perception. He or she must also prefer "yes, and…" to "yes, but…"
(10) Regularly, the Mediator gives the participants a list of emotions. People read out loud the words which best correspond to their current emotional state.

(11) The Mediator releases the participants only when the offender and the offended person have shifted from negative to positive emotions.
(12) Once done, the Mediator records in a notebook the origin of the conflict, who was involved, what was said, and what the outcome of the dialogue was.

On the second page of the notebook is attached a list of thirty feelings:

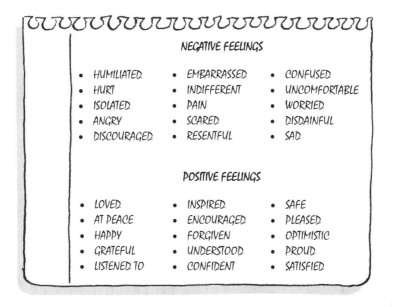

NEGATIVE FEELINGS

- HUMILIATED
- HURT
- ISOLATED
- ANGRY
- DISCOURAGED

- EMBARRASSED
- INDIFFERENT
- PAIN
- SCARED
- RESENTFUL

- CONFUSED
- UNCOMFORTABLE
- WORRIED
- DISDAINFUL
- SAD

POSITIVE FEELINGS

- LOVED
- AT PEACE
- HAPPY
- GRATEFUL
- LISTENED TO

- INSPIRED
- ENCOURAGED
- FORGIVEN
- UNDERSTOOD
- CONFIDENT

- SAFE
- PLEASED
- OPTIMISTIC
- PROUD
- SATISFIED

It appeared that everyone understood. I could even see in their eyes a certain yearning to test it. I was happy. On the next day, I came home late, and a bit tense. As we were eating, I teased Magali who didn't hesitate one second to ask for the Dialogue Table. The kids looked at us with a big smile, wondering what would happen next. I whispered to my wife that the Dialogue Table had been invented for the children, not for us. But she looked at me seriously and requested it again. I had no choice. I had to comply. We sat at the table, and asked for a Mediator. Liam, our youngest son – he was about seven at the time – came running and proudly sat in the Mediator's chair. He then conscientiously read out all the rules, and managed the facilitation of the dialogue perfectly, stopping us when we were both talking at the same time, accusing the other person instead of sharing our own perception, or when we were not correctly repeating what the other person had said.

We used the table in our family for about two months. I specifically remember one Dialogue Table with our oldest son. We were angry at one another for whatever reason. We sat at the table for nearly two hours! Noam tried several times to leave the table saying disdainfully "OK. I feel happy and understood. Can I leave?" The Mediator, Tom, his younger brother, reminded him of his commitment made on the day I bought the table, and refused to let him go, noticing that if the words were right, the tone and consequently the feelings were not. We kept on talking, and talking, and talking, one after the other. Listening. Rephrasing. Over and over, again and again. Until finally, after two hours, the nut cracked. We both started to cry, and felt into one another's arms.

In just a few weeks, the number of arguments between our children went from one a day, to one a week, to no arguments anymore (or very rarely). Some people have told me that it was because my children were afraid to sit for so long at the Dialogue Table. Maybe they are right. However, I prefer to believe that it is because they have fully integrated this respectful form of communication, and don't need the table anymore.

As I wrote this, I felt nostalgia for this intense moment of learning in our family. So I did some hunting around to see if I could find the Dialogue Table notebook. And I did. Here is the last entry:

"People involved in the conflict:
Noam, Tom, and Liam.

Reasons for the conflict:
Noam and Tom took their little brother by the feet and dropped him in the garbage.

Emotions at the beginning:
Liam expressed sadness, pain, and anger. Tom and Noam said they felt indifferent and disdainful.

Emotions at the end:
Liam said he felt peaceful, happy, optimistic, and listened to. Noam and Tom expressed satisfaction and gratitude. Noam, Tom, and Liam forgave one another and gave one another a big hug."

Deaf Tip n°4: Be sequential
Exercises

- Teaching others is the best way to learn. Share something you have learned in this chapter with at least three friends, colleagues, or members of your family.
- Pay attention to your inner dialogue for a full week. What do you do when other people are talking to you? Do you really listen to what they are saying? Do you pretend to listen but think about unrelated topics? Do you try to guess what they are going to say next? Or do you prepare what you want to say?
- Observe the way you interact with people for a week. Do you always let them finish their sentences? Do you interrupt them in the middle of their sentences to say what you want to say? Do you finish other people's sentences? If so, how much of their sentences do you finish? One, two, three words? For a full week, let people finish what they have to say, without interrupting them.
- Select a thought. How long can you concentrate on it? Try over and over again to focus on it longer.
- Sit in a comfortable place. Close your eyes. Remain in that position without moving or contracting a single muscle. Try to do this for at least 15 minutes.
- In order to help you focus on one thing at a time, take drawing lessons, or listen to classical music while visualizing each instrument as it plays.
- When you disagree with someone, try to start your sentences with the word *and* instead of *but*.
- Introduce the power toy technique to your team if you think it might be useful.
- Put into place the Dialogue Table at home if you think it can help your family.
- What could you do to improve your communication with the three people you selected in the introduction?
- Practice, practice, practice.
- Once done, move on to another chapter.

Personal Notes

Any intelligent fool can make things bigger and more complex.
It takes a touch of genius and a lot of courage
to move in the opposite direction.
Albert Einstein, German Physicist

Deaf Tip n°5
Be simple and precise

Because of Martin Luther King, Jr's words, 300,000 people marched on Washington to reclaim their civil rights. It was also with words that Adolf Hitler killed 50,000,000 people. Words might not be real, but the emotions and behavior they trigger certainly are. Words influence the way we feel, think, talk, and act. Words are never neutral. They always drive us towards more openness, cooperation, and pleasure, or towards more suspicion, isolation, and sorrow. The greatest sufferings we go through are never physical. These types of sufferings never leave hematomas, or broken bones, but they leave people crippled for life. Children will recover from slaps and smacks,[64] but none will survive the violence of hateful words spat by adults who ought to love and protect them.

One of my friends shared with me the following anecdote about his wife. They had been living together for more than twenty years and he had never understood why she was always so reluctant to get her driving license, to find a job, to meet new people, or to simply try new things. It was as if the only place where she felt safe was inside the four walls of their house, with him and with their three children. Then, one day, after twenty years of marriage, she opened up, and shared with him the root of her ill-being. When she was about fourteen – she does not recall exactly why, maybe because of not doing her homework, or not learning her lesson – the teacher made her stand in the middle of the classroom, and asked every single student to stand up and form a circle around her. Then, the teacher asked each student, one after another, to walk up to her, look her in the eyes, and say: "You're stupid! You're stupid! You're stupid!" According to what she recalls, every single student did it. No one had the courage to refuse. Thirty years later, this young girl, now in the body of an adult, was still doing her best to avoid being around people, and to avoid talking to anyone, she was so afraid of once again being wounded.

Even if we are not often confronted with this type of verbal violence, words still influence us on a daily basis for better or worse. They impact us by the way their meaning resonates in our mind, but also, more simply, by the sound which is produced when they are pronounced. Skeptical? Then, look at the following two shapes. Which one would you call *maluma*, and which one would you call *takete*?

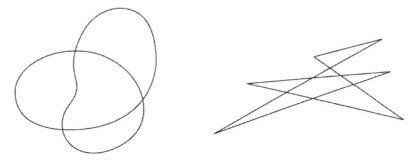

When people are asked this question, 90% of them call the star-like shape *takete*, and the cloud-like one *maluma*. A similar experiment was conducted with the words *kiki* and *bouba*, obtaining the same results. *Kiki* was consistently associated with the angular shape and *bouba* with the rounded one.[65] An association which is not limited to the adult world, as children under the age of 3 also link the same sounds with the same shapes.[66] Going even further, Spence, working with world renowned chef Blumenthal, has demonstrated that people not only associate shapes with specific sounds, but also with scents, textures, and even flavors. After having asked people to taste Brie cheese and cranberries, he asked them which of the two dishes was *takete* and which was *maluma*. The great majority of people associated cranberries with *takete* and Brie cheese with *maluma*.[67]

We sense letters like L, M, B as soft, and P, T, K as hard. We sense some words as negative, cold, and aggressive, and others as positive, warm, and pleasant, even when we don't have the least idea about what they mean, and even if these words don't even exist. Words resonate in us differently, and consequently induce different behaviors. In an experiment which has become a classic, Bargh, Chen, and Burrows showed how easy it was to prime the brains of people with simple words, and change their behavior. In this experiment, the psychologists gave students a fake language ability test. The test consisted of 30 sentences, each sentence made up of 5 words presented in an incorrect grammatical order. Students were asked to reconstruct each sentence in the correct order. Three versions of the test were used: one aggressive, one polite, and one neutral. In the aggressive test 15 out of the 30 sentences contained words such as *bold*, *disturb*, and *interrupt*. In the polite version 15 out of the 30 sentences contained words such as *respect*, *patient*, and *courteous*. Once done, the students were invited to go back to the waiting room, and ask for the second part of the test. In the waiting room, the man responsible for giving the document was talking to an accomplice who, with his back turned to the students, was timing how long it would take them to interrupt the conversation. What was the result? Less than 20% of the participants who had been primed with the polite list interrupted the conversation within ten minutes, while more than 60% of those who were primed with the aggressive list did. Three times more![68]

In a second experiment, the same scientists asked students to participate in a pseudo language proficiency experiment. With laser detectors, they recorded the walking speed of the participants as they arrived. A recording was made for each participant in the hallway over a walking distance of ten meters. As in the previous exercise, participants were asked to rearrange sentences containing scrambled words. One group was exposed to neutral words, the other to words referring to elderly stereotypes such as *Florida*, *old*, *wise*, *bingo*, *retired*, *wrinkles*, etc. Any word referring directly to slowness was excluded. Once done, the participants left by the hallway through which they had arrived, and their walking speed was once again measured. The result was that the participants who were asked to reorganize sentences linked to retirement not only walked slower than the participants in the other group, but also slower than when they arrived.[69]

Do you still believe that words are not important? That hanging around people who are vulgar, aggressive, or negative has no impact on you? Do you still believe that you are not influenced by the violent and sexual language of books, magazines, movies, commercials, songs, and video games? Knowing that words have such an impact on us, shouldn't we be more cautious and conscious of the words we hear and of those we use?

Simple and precise

When Deaf people communicate, they are both simple and precise at the same time. This is something that Hearing people have a hard time doing. When Hearing people try to be simple, they are automatically vague. And when they try to be precise, they suddenly become complex. If someone asks for directions, a Hearing helper will either be precise – Go down the street. At the second roundabout take the third road on the right. It's a small road. Pass the post office, a butcher shop with large windows, and a church with a red roof. At the lights take a left, then take the first road on the right... – so precise, that the person asking for directions will get lost, being unable to remember it all. Second possibility, the Hearing helper will try to remain simple –Straight ahead – and in this case, people asking for directions will once again get lost, this time because of a lack of precision. Hearing people can't be simple and precise at the same time. Deaf people can. They have this incredible ability to find the most economical way of conveying a complex message without losing any part of the information, a skill which has been recognized for centuries. In his *Trattato della pittura*, Leonardo Da Vinci already recommended that his apprentices learn the art of portrait from Deaf people because of their incredible ability to capture the essence of things. A lesson I learned firsthand myself.

One day, as I was coming back from India, I wanted to tell one of my Deaf colleagues that I had been training there. But I didn't know how to sign *India*, so I first drew a map of the world on the wall with my index finger starting with Europe, moving slowly towards the East until I drew a big triangle pointing downwards. The blank look in the eyes of my colleague confirmed what I already knew about my drawing skills. I then tried to come up with gestures representing Indian symbols: women's sarees, spicy tandoori chicken, sacred cows, beggars, fakirs, and snake charmers. Same blank look. Desperate, I shaped with my hands a house metamorphosing it slowly into the Taj Mahal. Suddenly, I saw a light in my Deaf colleague's eyes. Smiling, she took her index finger and placed it between her eyebrows, for the famous Bindi adornment, asking me to confirm. I had been so complex and so vague. She was so precise and so simple!

Be simple

Are Deaf people really better at keeping things simple? To find out, I asked Hearing and Deaf people to draw tricky words such as *philosophy*, *easy*, *friendly*, *lost*, *option*, *viewpoint*, etc. in less than 60 seconds. Here is a representative sample of the results I got for the word *Fall*.

Is it necessary to say that the Deaf drawing is on the left, and the Hearing one on the right?[70] The Deaf drawing is not only simpler than the Hearing one, it is at the same time more complete. While the Hearing drawing could be interpreted as a hunting scene, the Deaf drawing perfectly represents the season – the Fall – as much as the action – to fall – expressed by a spiral above the leaf. Two meanings in one single and simple drawing.

Lew: When I was a teenager, one day, our History teacher asked us to make a series of illustrations about WWII. We had studied it for several weeks. I had understood most of what the teacher had said, but had clearly missed most of the comments of my fellow students.

Bruno: So how did you manage to do your assignment?

Lew: The textbook we were using had seven chapters on the war, each chapter starting with a one sentence summary. So, I decided to make seven drawings, one per chapter, and then copy under the appropriate drawing the one sentence summary.

Bruno: And what did your colleagues do?

Lew: I was expecting them to do something long and complicated, and that's exactly what they did. Out of the 35 students in my class, not one did the same thing. The teacher showed my work to the whole class and gave me an A. I definitely think that a Deaf strength is the ability to keep things simple.[71]

Keeping things simple while not losing any information is something we desperately need in our over-connected world. There are more people today who have a Facebook account than there were people living in the world 200 years ago! With one click, we can send a message to an unlimited number of people. In 2010 an estimated eight trillion sms messages and 107 trillion e-mails were sent worldwide. And these figures are increasing every year. Who can cope with such a flow of information? One solution to fight this avalanche would be to limit the number of e-mails and SMS one sends a day, or the number of people one puts in copy. Another more feasible solution would be to write simpler e-mails. You have been asked by a manager to facilitate a one day workshop and you try to set up a date:

> Justin,
> I'm available on any of the following dates:
> - 6 November
> - 7 November or
> - 13 November.
> Would any of these three days suit you and your team?
> Many thanks,
> Ben

Look at the following two answers (the first one is a real e-mail I received). Which one would you prefer to receive?

> Dear Ben,
> I have checked the availability of my team. The last proposal, 13 November, appears to be the best. However, not all of them would be able to join. Paul and I are responsible for two seminars which are run in parallel, which means that we would have to step out of the workshop if there was an emergency. Mary and Clare would have problems due to workload at the welcome desk. And Alan cannot make it at all in November. Is there any reason to have this workshop in November? I would prefer to have it in December. Best regards,
> Justin

> *Thank you, Ben.*
> *I would prefer to have the workshop in December.*
> *Can you please suggest new dates?*
> *Regards,*
> *Justin*

Our communication should be simple, but not too simple. One day, I was sitting with my son, Liam, who was about six years old at the time. We were waiting for someone, and he was clearly getting bored. I put his little hand in mine, and squeezed it twice, expecting him to do the same back to me, which he did. I smiled, and he smiled. I did it again, this time squeezing his hand five times. He looked at me, and squeezed my hand back five times too. To vary the game, I changed the length and intensity of the squeezes, sometimes making them short and light, sometimes long and hard, and I explained to him that Morse code was based on this principle.

"What's Morse code, dad?" he asked.
"Before the telephone was invented," I explained, "people used Morse code, a sort of alphabet made up of short and long pulses to communicate over long distances."

Liam was listening carefully. So to illustrate, I explained that in Morse code, the word S.O.S. was made up of three short pulses for the S, three long for the O, and three short again for the second S. When the Titanic was sinking, I explained – remembering what my grand-mother had told me when I was a child – this was how they called for help. I put his little hand in mine and gave three short squeezes, three long ones, and then three short ones again.

"Do you understand?" I asked to see if my explanation was clear.
"Yes," he replied. "But whose hands were the people on the boat holding?"

In this case, my explanation was clearly too simple. So what about you? How do you express yourself? Do you write endless sentences or are you concise? Do you tend to be simple or complex? How many verbs do you use in a sentence? One, three, ten? Do you get short of breath when you talk? Have you ever witnessed anybody dozing while you explained something? How would other people describe the way you talk? Would they say that you get straight to the point, or that you beat around the bush? Do people have to make an effort to understand you? Or are you sometimes too simple?

Be precise

Look at the above picture. How would you describe it? Probably as follows: "A table with four plates, four forks, four knifes, and four glasses." This is a good description. It is simple. But it is not precise. Precise would mean that if someone was to draw the picture again, this time based on what you said, the result would be a drawing identical to the original one. This would not necessarily be the case with your description. Based on your description, there is a good chance that the new drawing would look like this:

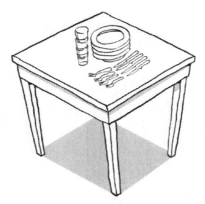

Why such a result? Because your description was correct, but not accurate. Precision is what makes something simple and correct become accurate. A mistake which would never occur in the Deaf world. With Deaf people, picture two would be the exact copy of picture one. Why? Because when observing picture one, Deaf people would naturally describe not only the objects, and their quantity, but also their spatial position, positioning each plate, fork, knife, and glass exactly as shown in the original picture.

Precision is an important part of Deaf culture. Let's take, for example, the basic greeting ritual. When Hearing people meet, most of the time one person asks *How are you?* to which the other replies *How are you?* both asking the same question, no one answering it. Sometimes, when Hearing people are more evolved, to the *How are you?* Question, the reply will be *Good!* even if in reality the person feels miserable. "Misnaming things adds to the world's misery" said Albert Camus. Why can't Hearing people tell the truth? Why do they avoid describing exactly how they feel when someone asks them? And why doesn't the person who asks the question see when the answer doesn't match the body language?

This form of greeting looks ridiculous compared to the precision of Deaf greetings. A Deaf person will ask you how you are by holding the hand closed, its back turned towards the floor, the index and middle fingers straight, pointing at you, then at him or her, moving the two fingers back and forth two or three times, a questioning look on his or her face. The Deaf greeter will then expect you to reply with the same sign, carefully observing the position of your two fingers and the muscle contractions in your face. If you feel overjoyed, you are expected to point your two fingers to 12 o'clock. If you feel OK, you point them to 3 o'clock. And if you feel down and depressed, then your fingers should be turned towards the floor, pointing towards 6 o'clock. In between these three positions, the gradation is unlimited, allowing you to express exactly your level of happiness or grief, by the precise direction of your fingers accompanied by the appropriate facial mimics.

Consequently, anyone can quickly and precisely see if you feel overjoyed (12 o'clock), great (1 o'clock), good (2 o'clock), OK (3 o'clock), tired (4 o'clock), anxious (5 o'clock), or depressed (6 o'clock), and because of this precision, like a concerned doctor, people can swiftly react in the appropriate way. This Deaf approach closely resembles the pain scale which has been used in hospitals for the last decade to identify the pain intensity in children or adults whose communication is impaired. With this self-assessment tool using ten descriptions of pain coupled with green to red emoticons, patients are more precise in describing their suffering and its evolution, and doctors can choose medications better, avoiding giving too much medicine to a whining patient, or not enough to a tough one. This is a bright approach which a friend of mine uses with his team. Having noticed that oral greetings were of no use, he has installed a white board at the entrance of the open space where his team sits. And every day, when team members arrive, they draw under their name a smiley, a skull, a lightning bolt, a heart, or anything else which represents their mood, and which can potentially evolve over the course of the day. It is difficult in this case to pretend that you are not aware that someone is going through a tough time.

So why do Hearing people have such a hard time expressing how they feel when they are asked? One of the reasons could be the paucity of oral language compared to Sign Language. Following a greeting, to avoid long sentences, Hearing people often think that they must choose between only two words: *good* or *bad* (or to be more precise, only one word, as the word *bad* is prohibited by good Hearing manners), a dichotomous language which is specific to the Hearing world. And if you think that you are different, if you believe that you don't see the world in black and white but in a whole palette of colors, then try the following exercise. In the chart below, write the middle ground between the two extremes, using only one word. Avoid words such as half-empty or half-closed, as they are not one word, and as they are not in the middle. Something which is half-empty is more empty than full, and something which is half-closed is more closed than open.

BLACK	GREY	WHITE
FULL	. . .	EMPTY
OPEN	. . .	CLOSED
HEAVY	. . .	LIGHT
HARD	. . .	SOFT
DARKNESS	. . .	LIGHT
CLEAN	. . .	DIRTY
FAR	. . .	NEAR
IN	. . .	OUT
AGILE	. . .	CLUMSY
NARROW	. . .	WIDE
INTELLIGENT	. . .	STUPID

And take your time

What then is the main block which prevents Hearing people from being like Deaf people, simple and precise? I believe it is *time*. Deaf people are able to remain simple and precise in their communication because of their continuous practice of this skill, but also because of their completely different attitude towards time. If you are a Hearing person, and if punctuality is important for you, be aware that Deaf people are not on the same time as you. Deaf people call it Deaf Standard Time (DST).[72] If you ever make an appointment with Deaf people, be sure to have a good book or some work with you as you might have to wait quite a while for them. Often Deaf people arrive late because on their way they met someone and couldn't resist the pleasure of stopping and chatting for a while. So, if they ever arrive on time, it is probably not on the right day.[73]

Boris: Deaf people can talk for hours completely losing the notion of time.
Bruno: This can also happen with Hearing people.
Boris: Maybe. But not to the same extent. One day, as I was going out for dinner, I bumped into a group of Deaf friends who were just leaving the restaurant I was going to. We had a short discussion, and then I entered the restaurant to enjoy my dinner. I remember having a full course dinner – three or four dishes – and when I left the restaurant more than one hour later, I found my friends still chatting in the very same place I had left them.
Bruno: That would indeed be unusual in the Hearing world!
Boris: You're right. While for us it happens frequently.
Bruno: How do you see Hearing people then, compared to you?
Boris: For us Hearing people always seem to be in a hurry. And when they say good bye, they mean it.
Bruno: Not Deaf people?
Boris: No. Not really. When Deaf people say good bye they take a few steps and then chat with someone else. Then, they say bye, stop again, and chat with another person. This ritual can sometimes last for several hours…

This behavior, which could be seen as a flaw in business, is definitively a plus in communication. As Deaf people always feel less in a hurry than Hearing people, they consequently take the time to explain things correctly – which is a prerequisite to being simple and precise.

In one of our courses, one of my Deaf colleagues wanted to explain to our trainees the meaning of the sign *September*. To make this sign in French Sign Language, you place your left hand at the level of your chest, with the thumb and the index finger forming a circle, and you use your right hand, in the same position, going three times from your left hand to your mouth. My colleague was trying to explain that the sign represented a French worker in a vineyard, during the harvest, tasting grapes. But the trainees didn't seem to understand. So my colleague quickly moved from iconicity[74] to mime, describing the scene. He mimed a man with a heavy basket on his back, facing a vineyard. He then described a long line of vines. And another. And another. Ten in all. Then, to show how large the vineyard was, he took the position of a Sioux scrutinizing the horizon, his right hand positioned horizontally at the level of his eyebrows, and remained in that position, for at least 5 seconds. I observed him in awe. He was so at ease with taking the time he thought it was necessary to explain it well. If I had been requested to do the same job, without a doubt, I would have described only one or two lines of vines, and remained in the Sioux position for no more than one second. I still can learn a lot from my Deaf colleagues!

Deaf Tip n°5: Be simple and precise
Exercises

- Teaching others is the best way to learn. Share something you have learned in this chapter with at least three friends, colleagues, or members of your family.
- We all tend to be either too vague or too complex when we talk. Observe yourself for a full day. Is it more difficult for you to be simple, or to be precise?
- Pay attention to what you say when you talk. Do you communicate with others or with yourself? Are you transmitting a message or are you structuring your thoughts by thinking out loud? If you tend to think out loud, next time you talk, try to do this part in your head, and speak out loud only when you are ready to really share something with others.
- When you write or talk, force yourself to structure each sentence with only one verb.
- Draw your face with no more than four lines. Once your pencil has moved away from the paper for the fourth time, you must stop. What stands out? Would someone recognize you? Do the same exercise with the three people you selected in the introduction.
- Next time someone asks you *How are you?* answer precisely how you feel, and as you do, observe the greeter to see if it was a real question.
- Watch the news on TV, and ask yourself after each topic what are the two key words which would summarize everything that was said. Do this exercise with a friend, and then, compare your results. Do this exercise regularly.
- Do the same exercise in your head during your next meeting and when people talk to you this week.
- Improve your ability to be simple and precise by building your vocabulary. Find a new word every week-end in the dictionary, and use it at least ten times in your conversations during the following week.
- What could you do to improve your communication with the three people you selected in the introduction?
- Practice, practice, practice.
- Once done, move on to another chapter.

Personal Notes

. . . .

. . . .

. . . .

. . . .

. . . .

. . . .

. . . .

. . . .

. . . .

. . . .

. . . .

. . . .

. . . .

Deaf Tip n°6
Don't say don't

The Financial Director of a high tech company came home late every day. His wife was tired of waiting for him, night after night, feeling lonely, raising the kids all by herself. Fed up, one evening, she said: "Honey, I don't want you to work so much!" On the following day, the man came home with a big smile on his face: "I thought all day about what you told me last night. I think you're right. I work too much. So on my way home, I stopped by a fitness center, and paid for a full year's subscription. From now on, I will leave the office early to go to the gym." If you don't say what you want, how can you expect people to know? Don't say what you don't want, say what you want because when you use primal language the impact you have on people is always more powerful.

Our primal language

Babies don't think in negatives. Not because they don't want to or have no opportunity to, but because they can't. Babies think in images, not in symbols,[75] for the obvious reason that they have not yet acquired a language structured around words.[76] During the first few months of our life we capture the world like an artist painting a blank canvas. I see Mom, I paint Mom. And when Mom is out of sight, the canvas remains blank. When Mom is gone, she stops existing as there is no visual correspondence to the symbolic words *no, nothing, never,* or *nobody*. The only way to paint the equivalent of "Mom is not in the room" is to paint a room. But how to know then where Mom is or what is missing from the room? No wonder that a baby cries when its Mom exists, doesn't exist, exists, doesn't exist. Anyone would go crazy for less than that. Hopefully, step by step, our right brain's visual language supports the development of a left brain's symbolic language to describe things which do not exist or which cannot be observed, like events which happened, will happen, or which have never happened or will never happen.

Years later, having turned into adults, most of the time we end up using a left brain symbolic and abstract language. In this paragraph, for example, only one word out of the one hundred and fifty five which compose it belongs to our primal language.[77] Nevertheless, despite our predominant left brain education, negative and symbolic sentences still require more time to be processed, leading to a higher rate of failures,[78] while messages formulated in our primal inborn language – sentences using concrete, visual, and positive wording – are understood better, more easily and faster.

A member of my team based in the Middle East told me about a moment of panic he had at the steering wheel of his car when he arrived at a customs checkpoint. The road suddenly changed into several lanes with above each of them a different prohibiting sign. One lane was forbidden for buses and trucks, another for cars and motorbikes, another for trucks and cars, etc. He was completely lost, afraid of causing an accident. When I asked him what was wrong, he naturally replied that guiding signs would have been more helpful than prohibiting ones: cars in this lane, trucks in that one.

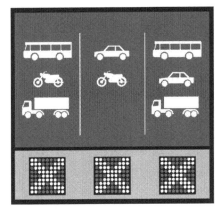 

It's the same when we talk. When we use negative words, just like the road sign on the left, people perceive our message as messy and overloaded with data. When we use positive wording, it becomes clear like the road sign on the right. Our brain is wired to work only with the positive. Still doubtful? Then try the following experiment: Close your eyes[79] and follow my instructions precisely: Don't think of an iceberg. Don't visualize an igloo on this iceberg. And please don't imagine a penguin being chased by a polar bear, running around the igloo which you do not see.[80] Did you follow my instructions? If you did, then you didn't see an iceberg, an igloo, a penguin, or a polar bear either. But the truth is that despite all your efforts to follow my instructions, in the last minute you visualized more polar landscapes than you will ever see in your entire life.[81] Why? Because to understand a negative message, we first need to visualize what is forbidden, put a symbolic cross on it, and then try to erase what is behind the cross. But it is too late. The brain has already recorded the image. And as the picture is concrete, while the cross is symbolic, as the picture is positive (do), while the cross is negative (don't), what happens? The cross disappears, and the picture remains.

When we formulate a negative request, we in fact invite the other person to do the exact opposite of what we want them to. Whenever you say to a child: "Don't fight with your brother," you give the order to the child's brain to fight. When a manager says to a team member: "Don't always complain," he or she encourages him or her to keep on complaining. And when I say to my spouse: "I swear! I didn't do it!" I suddenly become very suspicious. Here is a copy of a poster a colleague of mine found on the door of a classroom in a primary school. Can you guess how the kids behave in that school?

Once you understand how the brain processes data, you can play with it as much as you like. If despite all of your efforts, the project you have been working on for the past few months has been a fiasco, in this case it might be a good idea for you and your career to confess the truth this time with a negative sentence. Don't say: "My project was a failure" – your boss would only remember the word failure. Say: "My project was not an incredible success" and you never know, maybe you will get a promotion…

This is the reason why experienced hypnotherapists also prefer positive formulations to negative ones. With women in the early stages of pregnancy, for example, they will say "You feel completely relaxed. Your digestive system is functioning well," to avoid saying "You don't feel sick. You don't have any nausea," simply because they know that with the second formulation, they would only trigger in the patient's brain the desire to vomit, and, of course, they don't want this to happen, especially not in their office.

Without any formal training, Deaf people apply the same principle, in a very natural way. Because of the visual nature of sign languages, to keep it simple and precise,[82] and to make life easy for others,[83] Deaf people often tend to express in a positive way what Hearing people would say in a negative one. When Hearing people say: "Don't forget to post the letter," Deaf people sign: "Can you post the letter?" When Hearing people say: "Don't give up!" Deaf people sign: "Keep trying!" When Hearing people say: "Not bad," Deaf people sign: "Good." This is an essential difference. In these specific examples, while both cultures attempt to convey the same message, the Hearing brain records: forget, give up, and bad, while the Deaf brain records: remember, try, and good. Two forms of communication which will trigger two completely different behaviors.

Of course, just like with oral languages, sign languages also have a full range of negative forms of expression.[84] However, contrary to most oral languages, they don't have double negatives.[85] This figure of speech, called litotes, is based on the mathematic principle that two negatives cancel each another, resulting in a positive. No + No = Yes, "I don't disagree" meaning "I agree." This way of formulating a message is often used to cowardly say something without really saying it. The purpose of such a turn of phrase is that if you are ever accused of something, you can always say that you never said it, a dubious behavior which is definitely alien to the Deaf cultural habit of expressing what you think in a straightforward way.

For example, when someone offers a drink to a Hearing person, especially if it is alcohol, to reduce the risk of being seen as an alcoholic, they will often answer with something like: "Ich sage nicht nein," if they are Germans, "Je ne dis pas non," if they are French, or "I won't say no," if they are speaking English. By doing so, using two negative words in the same sentence, the answer sounds very much like "No, no, thank you, I never drink alcohol," when in fact it means: "Yes, please. I would really enjoy a drink." When you offer a drink to Deaf people the approach is completely different. If they want one, they will simply say "Yes." It is so much more honest, straightforward, and consequently easier to understand.

Another negative form of communication our brain has a hard time with is the overuse of *but*. How often do we use this word in a day? You would be surprised! "I agree, but…" "You've done a great job, but…" "I would like to, but…" "I'm fine, but…" "Maybe, but…" which means: "You've done a lousy job," "I don't want to," "I'm not fine," "No way." People know it. People know it so well that they often prefer to hear *no* than *yes but*. The word *but* immediately closes any possibility of dialogue, by passing a simple message: "There is only one truth: mine. I'm right. You're wrong."

What would happen if we replaced the negative word *but* with the positive word *and*? It would simply and powerfully reopen the dialogue between people, helping parties to explore new ideas, and search for new alternatives. What would you prefer to hear? "I agree with you, but…" or "I agree with you, and…"? Think about it. The first sentence creates negative feelings and ends any desire to collaborate further. With the second both parties are encouraged to exchange their points of view without criticizing each other, and to find a way to work constructively together.

It is worth mentioning that this *but/and* dilemma is specific to the Hearing world and is very different from the Deaf world. In Sign Language,[86] the sign for *but* is basically the same as the sign for *different*.[87] In other words, while in Oral Language *but* means "What has just been said isn't true," in Sign Language it means "There are multiple realities. We are different." The Hearing *but* closes any potential debate before it has even started, and pushes people to adopt fixed opposing positions. The Deaf *but* promotes exchange and complementarity. Do as Deaf people do, replace your *don'ts* with more efficient *dos*, and your *buts* with the much more respectful and collaborative *ands*. Then watch how people around you open up and share with you all sorts of new and interesting insights.

Positive thoughts produce positive behaviors

The way we talk to people has a direct impact on their behavior. Just like the way we talk to ourselves influences the way we behave. This is true even if we are not fully aware of the nature of our inner dialogue. This year, Noam, my oldest son, worked for the summer in a factory welding balconies. As the environment was noisy, he was required to wear earplugs, something he had never done before. When we talked at night about his first day of work, his comment was very interesting. "When I put the earplugs in, I started to hear my thoughts. I talk to myself nonstop. Dad! I didn't know I was talking to myself so much."

Becoming aware of our continuous inner dialogue is a good first step towards self-improvement. Knowing how we talk to ourselves is the next. What is the sum of our thoughts? More positive, or more negative? With more *dos* or more *don'ts*? More *buts* or more *ands*? It is hard to say with the constant flow of words we think and pronounce every day. A lesson a young man in search of spirituality learned after many years of effort.

Having heard about a monastic order which applied Saint Benedict's strict observance of silence, this young man thought that a silent retreat could serve his quest. In this monastery, monks had the right to speak only two words every two years. Despite his apprehension, the young man joined the religious order as a novice, and conscientiously followed all the rules imposed by their faith. After two years of silence, he went to the abbot's office to say his two words. He sat down, thought for a while, and then carefully said: "Food; Bad." Hoping that the food would improve, the young man went back to his austere cell in silent prayer. Two years later, he was again invited to speak two words. This time, he clearly knew what he wanted to say. He had thought about it for two full years. He carefully articulated: "Bed; Hard" and left happy, convinced that it would now improve the quality of his sleep. For two more years, the young novice devoted his life to God, fully committed to his vow of silence. Finally, came the long awaited moment of pronouncing two words again. This time, facing the abbot, the young man gravely and carefully pronounced the words: "I; Quit!"

"I knew you would," replied the abbot simply "you are always so negative when you talk!"

Hopefully, in real life we don't only pronounce two words every two years to know how positive or negative we are. It is simpler than that. People nourish the foolish belief that they can keep their thoughts secret. Nothing is further from the truth. No one can. A man who complains all the time about the weather or about his neighbors, is not describing so much his environment as the dialogue he nourishes inside his head. A woman who, at the end of dinner, says: "You don't want any dessert?" is not offering desert, but revealing that she has been hoping for the last hour that you will leave. People who conclude an e-mail with the sentence "Do not hesitate to contact me" are asking you to hesitate, and consequently reveal the fact that they don't want to be bothered. Every behavior, every sign, every spoken word starts with a thought. Whatever we say or do is first created in our mind. Thoughts crystallize into words, then into habits, and finally into circumstances.[88] People don't scream at, or talk disrespectfully to or about other people if they have not previously nourished thoughts of criticism and disregard towards those people. The words which come out of our mouths, and the behavior we adopt when in contact with people, are only the materialization of our thoughts. And according to their nature, these thoughts turn either into constructive or destructive interactions. If you want to know what people think, observe their behavior, and listen to the words they use. More importantly, if you want to know what type of thoughts you cultivate, become a better listener of the words you use, and a better observer of your own behavior. And if you don't like what you hear or see, then change your thoughts. Not your behavior, not your words, just your thoughts.

One thought at a time

Studies show that most of our thoughts are really only a few thoughts repeating themselves over and over again, and that the majority of them tend to be negative. We regret the past, blaming ourselves for things we did or regretting things we haven't done. We abhor the present, focusing on our weaknesses or comparing ourselves to others. And we fear the future, persistently worrying about the unknown.

To get rid of these negative thoughts, we must remember that if our brain is able to deal instantaneously with millions of pieces of data, it can focus on only one thought at a time. Not convinced? Then, take a look at the drawing above: the face of a liar.[89] How do I know it is the face of a liar? Because this face is also the word *liar* written diagonally. Now that you have seen both the face and the word, try to see both at the same time. If you pay attention to what is happening in your head as you do it, you will notice that it is impossible. The best you can do is to shift your attention from one thought (the picture) to the other (the word), engaging, focusing, disengaging. Engaging, focusing, and disengaging again. Moving from one thought to the other in just a few micro-seconds, being unable to see both simultaneously.

We cannot have two thoughts at the same time, just like we cannot have no thought at all. This is why it is useless to fight a thought, or to try to make it disappear. Something cannot be replaced by nothing. Natura abhorret a vacuo. Whenever you wish to get rid of a negative thought, the trick is not to fight it, but to replace or reframe it. You replace a thought by pushing it out, trading it for a stronger and more positive thought. You reframe a thought by giving it a new direction, a new meaning.

Replace

To be able to replace a thought you need to always have another one ready, a thought which is better and stronger. Knowing positive and uplifting songs, poems, and quotes by heart is a good way to have these thoughts at hand. Do you have depressing thoughts? Don't fight them. It is useless. Recite in your head a poem on courage, and your discouraging thoughts will go away. Do you have thoughts of hate or anger? Sing in your head a love song, and your hateful thoughts will disappear. But be cautious. You need to know them by heart. Just like a mantra, your quote, song, or poem must be said without hesitation; otherwise, your negative thoughts will use the blank space to creep back into your mind once again.

When I was a teenager, I learned a poem which often helped me when I was feeling down. It might not be the most sophisticated poem, but the message is right, and the length makes it perfect to fight negative thoughts and keep control of your mind's stage long enough. The poem is called *Invictus*, and was written by British poet William Ernest Henley. I would like to share it with you:

Out of the night that covers me,
Black as the Pit from pole to pole,
I thank whatever gods may be
For my unconquerable soul.

In the fell clutch of circumstance
I have not winced nor cried aloud.
Under the bludgeoning of chance
My head is bloody, but unbowed.

Beyond this place of wrath and tears
Looms but the Horror of the shade,
And yet the menace of the years
Finds, and shall find, me unafraid.

It matters not how strait the gate,
How charged with punishments the scroll,
I am the master of my fate:
I am the captain of my soul.

Reframe

If for some reason you cannot replace a thought, then you should reframe it. I learned about this technique by accident. One day, I was intrigued by a conversation I had overheard between two colleagues. One of them was telling the other that he loved traffic jams. I was shocked. How could anyone love traffic jams! I moved closer. "Why did you say you love traffic jams?" I asked. Without answering, my colleague pulled up the bottom of his shirt, and showed me his perfect six-pack abs. I was impressed, but couldn't make the link between traffic jams and his abs, so he explained it to me. "I heard one day on the radio the story of Guillaume Néry, the deepest man on Earth. Néry became a champion because at the age of 14, during his daily 45 minute trip to school, instead of dozing or talking to his friends in the school bus, he held his breath for as long as he could. I thought about it. I didn't like wasting my time in traffic jams, and at the same time, I didn't have time to go to the gym. So one day, I decided to combine the two. I designed a training program which could be done sitting in a car, focusing just on the abdomen." And, looking at his six pack, a big smile on his face, he once again uttered the shocking words: "I love traffic jams!"

This reframing approach was new to me, and it triggered my curiosity. At the time, I also had a problem with traffic jams, but my objective was not to look like a body builder. On the other hand, I was working on my PhD, and was often frustrated by the feeling that I didn't have enough time to think. So I decided to take a scrapbook with me, in the car, and every morning before starting the engine write a new question at the top of a page, and whenever I got stuck in traffic, instead of listening to nonsense gibberish on the radio, I would write down all the thoughts which came to mind concerning that question. A few days later, sitting at the steering wheel of my car, I was feverishly writing new thoughts in my scrapbook when suddenly the traffic light turned green. I nervously shouted "Oh no. Not yet!" And then, I realized how shocking what I had just said was. The reframing had worked. I had fallen in love with traffic jams! I shifted into first gear, and accelerated, a huge smile on my face.

Contrary to what most self-help books suggest, there are very few things we can change in our life. We can't change traffic jams. We can't change the weather. We can't change other people. We can't even control our own body. No one can decide to stop sleeping, to be in good health, or to avoid death, even if we can sometimes slightly influence these things. As Woody Allen said "if you want to make God laugh, tell Him about your plans." It is useless to spend time and energy on things we can't change. There is only one thing we can control in our life. There is only one thing we can change. It is our thoughts. "Forces beyond your control can take away everything you possess except one thing, your freedom to choose how you will respond to the situation."[90] This is the ultimate and only true freedom: the freedom to choose your thoughts.

It is by changing your thoughts that you change your life. You can adopt thoughts which either limit or expand your vision of the world, thoughts which build or destroy. These thoughts will then turn into words and behavior of the same nature. Let's imagine that you are on a diet, that you want to lose weight. You can either think "I'm too fat, I look like a cow," or you can think "I want to be slim; I want to weigh less than 70 kilos." Whenever you have a pang in your stomach, you can either think that you are hungry, that it is difficult, and that, like every year, you will give up before even seeing the first results. You can visualize all the good things you are missing: a table laid out with roasted chicken, crispy salads, hearty pastas, juicy red grilled meats, fresh vegetables, warm bread, chocolate fondue, cakes with lemon icing, ice-cream with hot fudge and whipped cream, and seasonal cocktails. If you do so, you will find yourself in front of the fridge without even knowing how you got there. Or, whenever you want to snack, you can visualize your future body: strong bones, young heart, healthy intestines, firm muscles, beautiful curves, silky skin, and a high level of energy. By thinking this way, you will find yourself less often in the cookie jar, and more often at the gym.[91] We are literally the sum of our thoughts. We never obtain what we want. Only what we think.

Is your head full of *don't, but, can't, forced to, won't last, only, again, always, never, impossible*? Then, it is time to talk to yourself and to others in a more healthy, constructive, and positive way!

Deaf Tip n°6: Don't say don't
Exercises

- Teaching others is the best way to learn. Share something you have learned in this chapter with at least three friends, colleagues, or members of your family.
- Improve the following expressions:
  "No act of kindness no matter how small is ever wasted."
  "Don't listen to anyone who tells you that you can't."
  "I don't regret my experiences because without them I couldn't imagine who or where I would be today."
  "You can't inspire others to do what you haven't been willing to try."
  "Don't bend, don't water it down, don't try to make it logical, and don't edit your own soul according to the fashion."
  "We don't love ourselves for what we are not."
- Keep on improving sentences for a full week whenever you read or hear a negative expression.
- Finish the following two sentences with whatever comes to mind, and feel the difference: "I will miss you, but…" "I will miss you, and…"
- Buy a counting clicker and count the number of times you use the word *but* in a day. On the following day start replacing the word *but* with the word *and*. And monitor daily if the number of *buts* reduces and your relationships with others improve.
- Wear ear plugs for one hour and pay attention to your internal dialogue. Write it down on a piece of paper. Are the words more positive or negative, inspirational or depressing? What are the most recurrent negative sentences you hear yourself say? With which positive expressions could you replace them?
- Select an uplifting poem, song, or quote, and learn it by heart.
- How much time do you spend a day on things you can control or influence? Make a list. How much time on things you can't? Should you change the ratio? If so, select one thing you should stop spending time and energy on and one thing you should start focusing on.
- What could you do to improve your communication with the three people you selected in the introduction?
- Practice, practice, practice.
- Once done, move on to another chapter.

Personal Notes

. . . .

. . . .

. . . .

. . . .

. . . .

. . . .

. . . .

. . . .

. . . .

. . . .

. . . .

. . . .

. . . .

No man really becomes a fool
until he stops asking questions.
Charles Proteus Steinmetz, German Mathematician

Deaf Tip n°7
Dare to ask questions

We were in Manchester for a friend's wedding. One of my sons asked me if we could go to the Abercrombie & Fitch store. I typed into my smartphone *Manchester+Abercrombie* and found: Buckland Hills Mall on Buckland Hills Drive. I entered the address into the car's GPS, and a list of street names appeared, one was Buckland Avenue. Close enough. Malls are more often on avenues than on drives. However, when we got there, it was a residential area with no mall around. I went back to my smartphone, and looked at the Mall on a map. Close to it there was a road called Ridge Road. I entered the name of the road into the GPS, and found a Ridge Walk close by which seemed to be right. But when we arrived, we were in the middle of the countryside. I started to have doubts. I looked at the address of the store again, this time more carefully, and I saw next to the name of the city two little letters I hadn't noticed before: CT. The mall was in Manchester, Connecticut, USA, not in Manchester, UK!

What did you say?

Such is life. To communicate with one another we use words to which we give different meanings. We talk about streets and avenues with the same name, but which are on different continents. In my communication courses I often write on a paper board the word *run* and ask trainees to individually write all the words which come to mind when they think about that word. Once done, I ask them, in sub-groups of four, to guess how many words they think they all thought of, how many words only two or three of them have in common, and how many words are unique, having been thought of by only one person in the group. With very few exceptions, groups believe that they have a lot of words in common and not very many which are unique. They are always amazed to discover, once they have counted and compared their words that they have on average more than 40 words which are unique, and not one single word shared by all.

ALAN	MARIE	SHANY	HAMID
SHOES	LEAVE	SPEED	CRAMPS
SPORT	ARRIVE	TOGETHER	WALK
FREEDOM	FAST	MARATHON	CHICKEN
ESCAPE	PLEASURE	RACE	MUSCLES
MUSCLES	HEALTH	WHERE	SWEAT
SPEED	UNWIND	END	NATURE
CATCH	DYNAMIC	RELAX	LAKE
TIRED	BASKET	AFRAID	LEGS
HEART	SWEAT	POLICE	FEET
PULSE	SUN	SNAKE	
	SNAKE	FALL	

One of my colleagues, a Project Management trainer, saw this exercise and was so impressed by the results that she asked me if she could do it using the words *Project Management* instead of *run*, in a course planned for the following week. I advised her not to do it. Certainly, experienced project managers working in the same company would all think about the same key words: time, cost, quality, milestones, go/no-go decision, risk, or lessons learned. She still did it.[92] And to my great surprise, she obtained the same results: not one single word in common despite the fact that these people had been working on the same projects for years, and shared the same corporate culture.

Yet, is it surprising? After all, no two people have or will ever have the same life experience. We use the same words, but give them completely different meanings. We are taught at school that we speak the same language, and that the meaning of the words we use can be found in the dictionary. This is a myth. For the word *home*, someone will visualize a loft in a skyscraper, other people will see a ranch, an igloo, a trailer, a log cabin, a yurt, a house made out of concrete, of brick, or of stone. There are as many different mental images for a word as there are people. This is the difference between connotation – the meaning people give to words – and denotation – the definition which is found in a dictionary. Denotation is only an attempt to build bridges between connotations, and consequently between people. When we talk, most of us try to use words which we believe others know, so they will understand us. But as we all give different meanings to the words, the only thing that people can understand is their interpretation of our words.

And if we think we can use past experience to help us, we are wrong again. With all the possible combinations one can make with the 600,000 words found in the English dictionary, most of the sentences we create have never been used by anyone before.[93] As demonstrated by stylometry, every single human being uses a personal, specific, and unique language, a sort of lexical DNA. Assuming that we understand people because they say things which resemble things that we have said before is an invalid assumption which can only lead to more misunderstandings, frustrations, and conflicts.

Madan: A few weeks after my arrival in the US, on the university campus, I saw on a bulletin board that a student was giving haircuts every Friday in the restroom for only one dollar. I needed one, so I put my name on the signup sheet, and on the following Friday went at the scheduled time to the dormitory lounge for my haircut. But after having waited for a full hour, nobody showed up.

Bruno: Wrong place?

Madan: That's what I thought. I was the only one waiting in the lounge. So I asked a student who was walking by where the restroom was, and surprisingly he pointed to the toilets! That's when the penny dropped. I had thought that a restroom was where people rested, like the lounge. I would have never thought that the toilets could have been called that.

Bruno: I guess that people can rest in strange places! Coming from India, did you often face these types of misunderstandings?

Madan: Very often. Americans for example don't sell garages during garage sales, and don't play with their feet when they play football. They don't put nuts in the dough of doughnuts, and pineapples are not made out of apples and pines. Americans don't live in their living rooms, and when a boy and a girl take their car to park, it is usually not to park.[94]

Bruno: I know, I had the same problem. Guinea pigs don't come from Guinea and are not pigs, French fries are Belgian, alarms go off when they go on, and noses run while feet smell! It can indeed be a bit confusing for non-English native speakers.

This communication gap which is so visible between people belonging to different cultures is as wide between people who share the same culture but come from different family, professional, educational, philosophical, or religious backgrounds, except that in this case the misunderstandings are even more pernicious as no one suspects there to be any difference. Communication is so much a part of our lives that we don't think about it anymore. We talk like we eat or walk. It is only when we sprain an ankle, come back from the dentist, or meet a foreigner that we suddenly realize that these actions – walking, eating, and communicating – are not easy or natural at all.

To ask or not to ask, that is the question

Confronting the same source of misunderstanding, the Hearing and the Deaf worlds have developed different strategies. Hearing people usually stop asking questions at around the age of five[95] when self-consciousness becomes predominant. It is around this age that Hearing people develop, for some reason, the belief that asking questions is a way of showing inferiority, weakness, and incompetence.

Kimy: At University, when I'm in an auditorium – with the help of an interpreter – I often raise my hand to ask questions.
Bruno: And the fact that you constantly stop the flow of the course doesn't bother the other students?
Kimy: I don't think so. In fact, I think it's more the opposite. Often, Hearing students come to see me after a course and say: "Hey, thank you for having asked that question. It was great."
Bruno: And what do you reply?
Kimy: I ask them: "Why didn't you ask the question if you didn't understand?" And their answer is always the same: "Oh, no. I can't. I don't dare to. There are too many people in the auditorium."
Bruno: So?
Kimy: So, I don't understand. I just don't get it. For me it's always very surprising. When you don't understand something, you should ask, right? Personally, I couldn't remain silent. I need to understand, I need to learn.

This Hearing behavior – avoiding asking questions – can be observed as frequently at school as in the corporate world. Often, in important meetings, Hearing people silently torture themselves: "Everyone seems to understand. Everyone except me. Should I say so? I'd better not. They'll think I'm stupid. They might even laugh at me. OK. I'll act as if I understand. Let's nod the head, like the others. Yes, but what if someone asks me a question?" Hearing people think that asking for clarification is a sign of submission. They behave as if they understand everything, hoping that more information will shortly help them catch up. They bluff, letting others think that they are up-to-date. But soon, it is too late. They reach a point of no return where they cannot confess anymore that, since the beginning, they haven't had a clue about what is going on. And if a courageous colleague ever dares ask for clarification, once received, if he or she still does not understand, that colleague will behave as if it was clear that time, never daring to ask a second time. Hearing people would rather leave a meeting or an interview clueless than take the risk of being seen – they think – as incompetent. Not so with Deaf people.

Lew: A few months ago, the producers of a TV show called our company to ask for our support in one of their marketing campaigns. My boss and I flew to New York to meet with them in order to understand their request.
Bruno: How did you communicate with them?
Lew: By reading their lips. It's not easy of course, but by focusing intensively and interrupting from time to time to ask for clarification I can manage. However, at the end of the meeting, I said that there were one or two points which remained unclear for me and that I wanted to ask a few questions.
Bruno: And I guess it made your Hearing boss nervous…
Lew: You're right. He said out loud in front of our potential clients that he had understood it all, showing me his notes.
Bruno: So?
Lew: So I took a quick look at his notes and didn't find the answers to my questions. On the following day, when we were back in the office discussing our assignment, we quickly disagreed on what our new clients really wanted. After I insisted for a full hour, he finally agreed to call them to ask for clarification. Once he hung up, he looked at me disconcerted and said: "How do you do that?" Well, apparently, it's not because you hear that you understand [smile].[96]

To avoid misunderstandings Deaf people often apply a two-step approach. Step one: they repeat everything several times, each time from a different angle. Something like: "It's a little house… a small house… it doesn't have many rooms… smaller than most houses…" Step two: they ask a whole series of questions after each interaction: "Was I clear? Do you have a question? Do you want me to repeat?" And for a Hearing person, one of the most surprising questions Deaf people ask is: "Can you please repeat what I just said?" followed by intense concentration on reformulation, and then confirmation or fine-tuning if necessary of what has been repeated. Such careful transfer of information from one person to another is rarely found in the Hearing World.[97]

The first time I observed this form of communication, it felt odd. My knowledge of Sign Language was very basic and a Deaf colleague was explaining something to me with many signs I didn't know. I was trying to grasp the general meaning but was having some problems. After having reformulated her message in different ways, she stopped, and signed:

Aloha: Was I clear?
Bruno: Yes. Yes. Very clear! Thank you.
Aloha: Did you understand?
Bruno: Yes, yes. Of course.

Aloha: Can you please repeat what I said?
Bruno: Err…[98]
Aloha: [Upset] Why are you telling me you understood when you didn't? Why won't you ask a question?
Bruno: Well. I didn't want to stop you.
Aloha: What's the use of talking to you if you are only pretending to understand?
Bruno: Well. I guess that I didn't want to feel stupid.
Aloha: In my culture, it's not people who ask questions who are stupid, it's people who don't![99]

Don't ever lie to a Deaf person, you will always look stupid.[100] That day I learned an important lesson: when you don't understand something, ask questions.

Why such a cultural difference?

Why such a difference between the Hearing and the Deaf worlds? Why are Deaf people so at ease with asking questions all the time? One explanation might be that they have no other choice if they want to survive in a Hearing world. Another explanation – which I believe is more valid – is that this constant questioning is linked to the nature of Sign Language. The written form of a language has the effect of slowing down its evolution, and contrary to most languages, Sign Language has no written form. Consequently, without this written anchor, Sign Language evolves faster than any other language. Imagine two Deaf friends who share the same Sign Language. They live in the same city and meet and communicate on a regular basis. If one of them was to move to another city for a few months, even if it was in the same country, and if the Sign Language used in both cities was the same, when they met again they would discover that some of their signs had evolved differently. Faced with this situation, they would have no other choice than to ask each other many questions: Can you please repeat? What is that sign? What does it mean? Can you explain? Can you sign it differently?

When I started to take French Sign Language lessons, the sign for October was made by placing the tip of the thumb against the tip of the other fingers, forming an O shape, moving the hand into a circle. Six months later, during a conversation, a Deaf colleague referred to a month, signing it with the tip of the thumb touching the tip of the index, the other fingers open, pointing to the sky, the hand moving down in a vertical wavy way. I asked:

Bruno: What month is that? It's not one of the twelve that you taught me. Is there a 13th month that I don't know about?

Amethyste: [Smile] This is the sign for October.

Bruno: October? But you taught me six months ago that the sign for October was an O moving in a circle!

Amethyste: I know. But since then it has changed.

Bruno: Who changed it? When did you change it? Why did you change it?

Amethyste: Well, it's difficult to say. Signs evolve all the time. Naturally. If people understand them, like them, and accept their evolution, then they relay them until the whole Deaf community uses them.

Bruno: And if they don't like them?

Amethyste: Then these new signs quickly disappear.

Bruno: So why did people adopt this evolution of October?

Amethyste: This new sign is more complete than the previous one. The O of October is still present, but now you also have the shape of a chestnut falling from a tree. And people liked it.

For someone like me, coming from an extremely slowly evolving language, this was a shock. But I now understood more clearly why Deaf people ask questions so often and why they are so comfortable with doing so.

The power of questions

Hearing and Deaf people are programmed the same way. No human being is able to ignore a question. When a question is asked, we automatically become captivated by it until we find an answer which releases us from it.

When I visited Istanbul's Blue Mosque, strolling through its well-tended garden, a surprising interaction between two men caught my attention. A Turkish peddler wanted to sell some postcards to a tourist. The tourist was becoming increasingly angry at the peddler, but for some reason seemed at the same time glued to him. Why didn't he walk away if he didn't want to buy something and if the interaction was irritating him? Because every time the tourist turned around to leave, the peddler asked him another question: Where are you from? What are you looking for? Do you like Turkey? And as if by magic, the tourist stopped, turned back, looked at the peddler again – in an even more irritated way – and answered the question (which was in fact a hook) as if walking away without answering was too painful for him. Once the question had been answered, the peddler tried to sell his trinkets again. The tourist would then turn away, the peddler asked a new question, the tourist stopped and answered, and the peddler went back to his sale's pitch. A fascinating dance!

Any inquisitorial body – sales people, journalists, policemen… and children – knows this. The most efficient way to convince, influence, or control people is not by asserting but by asking questions. The first reason for this is that a question can never be wrong, but an answer can. The second is that only the person who is answering the question is under the spotlight, and becomes vulnerable because of the pressure. If you are ever interviewed by a journalist, and if you want to have some fun, when he or she asks you a question, ask a question in return, and then, enjoy the confusion.

Terry: When I was in primary school I would easily get mad when a teacher spelled my name wrong. Whenever they wrote Terry with a *y* I would pay attention to them, participate, smile, and even give them home-made presents.
Bruno: And if they didn't spell it right?
Terry: Well… If they spelled Terry with an *i* I would make them pay for it.
Bruno: How?
Terry: Whenever they talked to me I would only reply with a whole series of "Huh? What did you say? Can you repeat?" until they felt miserable.[101]

Asking is obviously more powerful than telling. No progress was ever made without a question first. Every scientific discovery was made by someone who had previously wondered about something. Every spiritual revelation was given to someone who had enquired about the Divine. Every social revolution was achieved by someone who questioned the system.[102] Whenever we learn something new, it is because first we had a question in mind. This is the reason why it is useless to give feedback to anyone who has not requested it. And even when people request it, it is best not to tell them what you think or have observed, but to make them talk, through questions. When we talk, people don't listen. They prepare what they are going to say next. When we ask questions, people have to listen and think. Good teachers (managers, educators, and parents) are experts at this. They know that it is only when they are in questioning-mode – not in telling-mode – that the people they are responsible for grow.

If you want to grow, don't wait for people to ask you questions or to give you feedback. Do it yourself. Ask yourself the right questions. But be cautious. If not asking any questions will stop you from making progress, asking yourself too many questions will have the same effect. A healthy habit is to always have one question in mind, no more, no less, and to focus on it until you find the answer before moving on to the next question. For some questions this process could take a day, for others it might take a year or even longer. But who cares? Personal development is not in the destination, but in the journey.

No stupid questions

During our years at school we learn to give correct answers to questions like: What is the capital of Bulgaria? Y=log X. If Y=10. What is X? – but we never receive any training on how to ask questions. And contrary to what people think, it is easier to find a correct answer than to ask a correct question. People say there are no stupid questions. Maybe. However, some questions are more effective than others. If you are thirsty and want a glass of cold water, you could ask any of the following questions:

1) Isn't it hot today?
2) Isn't water the best thirst-quenching drink?
3) Do you have something to drink?
4) Can I have a glass of water?
5) Can you give me a glass of cold water, please?

To the first question, your host might answer by talking about the weather. The second question is not a question, but an assertion. You are not asking something, but telling something. To the third question, in the worst case, you will only get a yes. Nothing else. In the best case, you might get a drink, but it might be a sugary soda, or hot coffee. To the fourth question, you might get water from the tap at room temperature. Only with the fifth question, because of its precise, polite formulation, will you get the glass of cold water you are longing for so much.

A few years ago, American journalist Thomas Friedman asked in a provocative article if Google was God.[103] It is indeed a question worth asking. Just like God, Google is everywhere, sees everything, remembers everything, and can answer any question, for anybody at any time of the day or night. And just like God, Google answers any question, as long as it is formulated correctly. We all have been in the situation of typing a few key words into a search engine and getting a lot of results, except the one we are looking for. We try again, with other key words. No luck. We think. We try over and over again. And then, suddenly, we think about new key words. A word combination we hadn't thought of before. We type them feverishly, and oh! a miracle! out of a myriad of data, the answer we were looking for suddenly appears before our eyes.

This important principle of asking the correct question works as much with Google as in our professional, personal, social, and even spiritual lives. When my wife was in her early twenties, she decided to go on a compassionate mission. She filled out the paperwork and prayed sincerely every day expressing her desire to go to an island. She wanted to help people, but she also wanted to do so in a nice sunny environment, with beaches, palm trees, and the sea close by. She understood that she had not been precise enough in her prayers when she received her call to indeed serve on an island, but without palm trees or coconuts: England. Be it with God, other people, or even with yourself, if you ask a vague question, you will get a vague answer. And if you ask the wrong question, you will get the wrong answer. The only way to get a correct and precise answer is by asking a correct and precise question.

To understand how to ask yourself a correct and precise question, you need to be familiar with the *but why?* technique. This approach, which is often used by Quality Engineers in root cause analysis, consists of examining a problem by asking a question in order to find its cause. Every time an answer is given, another *but why?* question is asked. Let's imagine that you are a School Principal and that the number of drop-outs in your school is increasing. Shouldn't you ask yourself the question *but why?* Once you come up with an answer (e.g., the teachers are not interesting enough), probe the answer with another *but why?* question, to which you will get another answer (e.g., teachers lack motivation). Repeat the process again and again, until you can't find another answer to the last *but why?* you asked. When you reach this level, there is a good chance that you will have found the root cause of the problem, and consequently the first switch to improve the situation.

Finding the question you should ask yourself works along the same lines. You can be sure that the first question which comes to mind will never be the right one. Just like a Russian nested doll – revealing a series of smaller dolls of the same sort inside – your initial question certainly holds many other questions. Which is the one you really need to ask yourself? Traditionally there are 5 nested dolls in a matryoshka. Apply the same rule. Refine your question using the sentence *what do I really want to know?* at least five times. Suppose one of your team members is aggressive. What do you really want to know? Maybe what is provoking this aggressivity? But this is not the right question. You still have at least four additional rounds to go through before reaching the right question. If you think that you are the cause of his frustration, then ask: *What do I really want to know?* Maybe you want to know what is it that you say or do which triggers these negative emotions in him? Let's imagine that the answer which comes to mind is the pressure that you've put him under during these last few weeks. Then, ask again: *What do I really want to know?* Move through this process until no clear and rapid answer comes to your mind.

Once you have reached this point, write down the question on a piece of paper, and place it somewhere where you can regularly see it (e.g., a post-it on your computer or a note on the fridge). Then relax, and let your brain do the rest. The answer will pop into your head when you least expect it, during the night, in the shower, or while driving. And if your brain does not produce an answer, it either means that the question was not the right one – if so, you should go through the *what do I really want to know?* process again – or it means that your brain doesn't have the answer. In that case, you need to shift from asking yourself the question to asking someone else.

And to ask someone else a correct question, three conditions are required: first, precision (see the previous chapter), second, honesty, and third, space. Honesty means that you truly have something to ask. It means that you are looking for information you don't have. Your objective must not be to transmit a message ("Don't you think that…"), and even less to boast by camouflaging – but not too much – your superior knowledge behind a fake question. Your objective must really be to acquire new knowledge. More often than not, our questions are not real questions. They often tend to focus more on ourselves than on others. So, how can you be sure that you are really asking a question and not showing off? Simple. Be aware that the more long-winded you are, the less you are in questioning mode. A real question is expressed in one sentence, using only one verb, and starting with the words: who, what, when, where, why or how. Anything more is a way to garner people's attention. The third condition, space, means that once you have asked your question, you stop talking, completely, and leave space for the other person to answer.

Several months after a course, a manager came to see me: "Your course with the Deaf facilitators completely changed my life." I thought the comment was a bit extravagant, so I asked him why he said that. "When I went on that course," he said "I was close to being fired. Working with Deaf people made me understand that I had a problem with questions. I never asked my team any questions. And as a result, no team member ever asked me any questions. After the course when I decided to ask genuine questions, being very careful to always be sincere, and to have the time and energy to concentrate on and listen to their answers, it completely changed the spirit of our team. It's just as if, by asking them questions, I have also given them the permission to ask questions to one another, and to take the time to answer them. I also learned to admit freely when I don't know, or don't understand something. This helped us share our different points of view, clarify our thoughts and understanding. The change in my team was so radical, that other teams saw it and asked us what was happening. Managers several levels above me were also interested in what was happening. Then, instead of being sacked, I got a promotion, and I received a pay raise. I even received a bonus! Last week, I got a call from a Head Hunter for a management position in another company. I told my boss, who is now making me a better offer to keep me on his team. All these changes because one day, Deaf people taught me that I could say "I don't know," "I don't understand," "Can you please explain it to me?"

When you don't understand something, or when you want to get back in control, don't talk. Don't say anything. Think. And then, ask a question. Dare to ask a question. But not any type of question. The right question!

Deaf Tip n°7: Dare to ask questions
Exercises

- Teaching others is the best way to learn. Share something you have learned in this chapter with at least three friends, colleagues, or members of your family.
- Try the *run exercise* with your team or with your family. Do it with a word you regularly use, and then talk about the differences. Where do they come from? From what life experience?
- When you watch a debate on television, or a street interview, listen carefully to the journalist's questions. Are they real questions? Or are they trying to force people to say what they want to hear?
- In your next three meetings, ask one question about a word, an idea, or a comment you don't understand. Then, see if your behavior encourages others to do the same.
- At the end of the next meeting you chair, or facilitate, instead of concluding with "Do we all agree?" ask people, one by one, if they need clarification on something you have been discussing, or even better, ask them to reformulate a specific topic.
- Next time you are angry with someone, don't express your frustration. Ask questions to better understand the other person's point of view. Then, think about the interaction. Was it more constructive and more productive than having an argument?
- Think about the last time you were misunderstood. What did you say? How could you have reformulated it in two different ways?
- For a full hour (or for a full day if you dare) when you talk, only ask questions. Nothing else.
- What is the one most important question you should ask yourself in the coming days? Write it down on a piece of paper and place it somewhere where you can see it regularly. If you don't have a question, here are a few suggestions: If today was the last day of my life, what would I do? What is the one fear that is holding me back? When is the last time I should have spoken up but didn't? If I had to change one thing in my life, what would it be? What can people learn from my life? What mistakes do I repeatedly make?
- What could you do to improve your communication with the three people you selected in the introduction?
- Practice, practice, practice.
- Once done, move on to another chapter.

Personal Notes

. . . .

. . . .

. . . .

. . . .

. . . .

. . . .

. . . .

. . . .

. . . .

. . . .

. . . .

. . . .

. . . .

*Now is the most important time
because it is the only time we have any power over.*
Leo Tolstoy, Russian Novelist

Deaf Tip n°8
Focus on the right thing

As I write this chapter, I'm 30,000 feet in the air on my way to Beijing, flying with Lufthansa. Since our take off, the cabin attendant has been calling me *Herr Dr. Kahne* and, as I flew out of Frankfurt, and have a German sounding name, she has been speaking to me for the last three hours in German. I don't speak a word of German, so I smile, guess what she is saying by reading her body language, and systematically answer in English. "Wollen Sie mehr mineralwasser?" she asks me in German, a bottle of sparkling water in her hand. "Yes, thank you," I reply politely in English, holding up my glass. I would think that as I am systematically answering her in English, she would end up speaking to me in English, as she does with all the other non-German passengers. But apparently she has decided that I am German, so she continues speaking to me in German.

Focus on the other

During the last decades many communication models have been proposed, most of them incorporating in some way the following elements: someone, called *the sender*, tries to communicate through sound, silence or body language with someone called *the receiver*. His or her communication, labeled *the message* is mainly composed of three elements: (1) the objective of the communication which often remains hidden, at least partially, in the mind of the sender, (2) the message which is actually expressed by the sender, and (3) the emotions which modulate the strength and direction of the message. Whatever the message, the quality of the interaction is often hindered by interference coming from the aural or visual environment (a motorbike driving by, the TV turned on), by the mental availability of the sender and/or the receiver (being tired, having an intense internal conversation), by their behavior (doing something else while communicating), or more simply, by their mood which, like boredom, stress, guilt, despair, fear, and anger, can greatly reduce their ability to focus.

A final difficulty we have to overcome if we want to connect with someone else is the filters that we have developed over our lifetime; a whole set of beliefs and values which we have incorporated through family upbringing and schooling, through culture, politics, philosophy and religion, through all the do's and don'ts imposed on us by the media, our peers, and society, until it becomes practically impossible for us to really express what we think orally ("Mom, Dad I love you") or hear what people try to tell us ("Your life is the way it is because of your own decisions, no one else's").

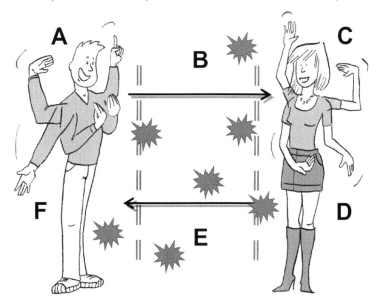

Consequently, the thought A going through the filters of the sender becomes sentence B, which through the decoding process of the receiver's filters becomes thought C. Thought C is then transformed during an internal dialogue to prepare an answer into thought D which once through the filters of the receiver who is now the sender, becomes sentence E. Sentence E goes though the filters of the original sender, now the receiver, and becomes thought F. At this moment, the original sender unconsciously compares thought A which was originally sent to thought F which has just been received, and emotionally says: "But, that's not what I said!"

Once we understand this process, a question naturally comes to mind: which filter is the most important? Or, to put it differently, whose filter should we focus on more to limit the distortion? Our own filters – making our words as close as possible to our thoughts? Or their filters – which requires knowing people so well that we can formulate what we wish to say in such a way that it will not be blocked or transformed by their filters?

To find out, I have run the following experiment more than fifty times. Twenty people who have never been in contact with Deaf people are told that they will be taught forty signs in 15 minutes, and that after, they will have a test to see if they can recognize seven sentences in Sign Language. This announcement visibly provokes excitement (learning signs) and anxiety (will I succeed?). Whatever the native tongue of these participants, a Deaf facilitator teaches them the numbers 1 to 21, the 7 days of the week, and the 12 months of the year in French Sign Language. Once done, 10 participants, called Group A, receive a blank sheet of paper (to force them to focus on the facilitator: the sender). The other 10 participants, called Group B, receive a sheet of paper with seven multiple choice answers (to force them to focus on themselves: the receiver). So group A writes down the date which the facilitator signs while Group B chooses the correct answer from 4 possible answers. What Group B doesn't know, however, is that 5 of the 7 multiple choice answers they have on their piece of paper have only incorrect answers, even if these somewhat resemble the date given by the facilitator (e.g., Monday 5 June, instead of Monday 15 June). The result of this experiment is striking. When the date given by the facilitator has the correct answer in the multiple choices, Group B always beats Group A. But when the date given by the facilitator does not correspond to any date given in the multiple choice answers, Group A always beats Group B, whose members choose an incorrect answer, even if they feel that something is wrong. Only 1 out of 10 people dares to challenge the four choices they have in front of them, and writes a fifth answer, the one they see the facilitator sign.

This is the story of our life. We all have a map of the world in our head, and as formulated by Korzybski, the map is not the territory. Sometimes this map corresponds to our environment, but most of the time it doesn't. Sometimes, the roads and buildings we have on our map match what we see, hear, and feel, but often we see roads which are not on our map, or we have on our map roads which we just can't find in reality. And whenever this happens, just like with the participants of the exercise described above, our reaction is: when reality does not correspond to our map of the world, it is never the map that we challenge or change, it is the reality. And how do we change reality? Simply by forcing people to say what we want to hear or by hearing what we want to hear even when people have not said it.

Not so long ago, I went to a school fair with my youngest son. After having tried most of the activities, Liam asked me if he could have an ice cream cone. There was an ice cream booth nearby so we walked up to it. The lady in charge looked at my son who has clear blue eyes and had long blond hair at the time, and said:

"What flavor does the young lady want?"

"I'm not a girl," said Liam "I'm a boy."

"Oh, I'm so sorry. See how we are? When someone has long blond hair and clear blue eyes, people think it's a girl. But of course, you're not a girl. You're a boy!"

Then, trying to make up, she said:

"And, what's your name, young man?"

"My name is Liam."

"Guillaume![104] What a nice name!"

We often believe that because we can talk, we can communicate. This is far from being true. Communication is more in listening than in talking, more in the unsaid than in the spoken words or in the signs. Yet, it is so hard to step out of our comfort zone that we prefer to hear what we want to hear, and to understand what we are used to understanding, than to listen to what other people are really saying, to avoid the risk of having to face a new reality. "People don't want to hear the truth because they don't want their illusions destroyed," said Nietzsche.

When we communicate we should clearly focus more on the other person than on ourselves. However, to do so, we first need to be aware of our filters. We need to be conscious of their distorting effects, and we must do everything possible to put them aside, at least for a short while, in order to really listen to the other person with a blank sheet of paper in front of our eyes. If before talking to someone, you believe that your map of the world is correct, and the other person's is wrong, cancel your interview or meeting. It will only be a complete waste of time and energy for everybody.

Focus on the meaning

Once we focus more on others than on ourselves, we can focus more on what they mean than on what they say. This is what we instinctively do with foreigners, paying more attention to what they are trying to say than what they are actually saying. This helps us avoid a lot of problems. During my last trip to China, a manager complimented me (I think) on a project I had just completed by telling me that I had done "a sexful job!" I hope he meant "a successful job." Along the same lines, when we were living in the USA, my wife always provoked interesting reactions when she was buying shits for the beds (in French the long *ee* sound does not exist). Focusing on meaning instead of words is of course less fun, but definitively more efficient. This is true with foreigners as well as with people who speak the same language as illustrated by the following story:

A man was walking on a beach with his young daughter. The sunset made to the sea a beautiful mix of pinks and blues. Wild horses were playing nearby. Touched by the beauty of the scene, the little girl took her father's hand and said: "Look, Daddy. The mommy horse talk to her baby." The father observed his daughter with much gravity and then, with a serious voice replied: "Honey, a mommy horse is called a mare, a baby horse is a foal, and horses don't talk, they neigh. Also, when the action is taking place you must use the present continuous and say the mare is neighing." The child was talking about beauty and love, the father about grammar and syntax. The child was focusing on meaning, the father on words.

How often do we focus more on words than on meaning? A team member is talking about his worries while the manager is focusing on Key Performance Indicators. A mother wishes to discuss the children's education while the father sees only the cost. If your child tells you that you have never loved him/her, who cares if you can prove them wrong? What is important is not what the child said, but why he or she said it.

Lew: My friends say that I can not only read their lips, but also their minds.
Bruno: Why do they say that?
Lew: I think they are referring to the most important skill Deaf people must acquire if they want to read lips, which is to focus on meaning. When I read lips, I can capture from zero to one hundred percent of the words pronounced. But it doesn't matter.
Bruno: It doesn't matter? Why?
Lew: Because you can capture all the words and miss the meaning. And you can capture only a few words and perfectly understand what the other person wishes to say. What's really important is not to understand the words, but the message. This is as true for Deaf people as it is for Hearing people.[105]
Bruno: You're right. When people focus more on what we say than on what we mean we suddenly become cautious of every word we pronounce. We hide behind our barricades and take no risks. Nothing fruitful can come out of such interactions.

One evening, Tom took an essay he had written for his French class out of his schoolbag and said: "Look, Dad!" I could see by the look on his face and the tone of his voice that he was happy and proud. And indeed, he should have been. On the top left corner of the essay, there was an encouraging comment from his teacher with a big mark of 18/20. He wasn't used to getting marks this high. Nor were we. I took the paper in my hand and said with a big smile: "Good job, Tom!" To my great surprise, his answer was harsh:

"How do you know that I did a good job? You haven't even read my essay…" He was proud of the work he had done, not of the mark he had received. I had focused on what was important for me, not on what was important for him. I had paid attention to the words, not to the meaning.

Focus on the here and now

Once you focus on others more than on yourself, once you focus on the meaning more than on the words, the last step is to focus on the here and now. What did you eat last night? What did you wear two days ago? Who is the last person you talked to apart from your family? And what did you talk about? If you are unable to answer to these simple questions, it means that even if you were physically present, your mind was somewhere else. This trend is more and more common in our society. When I go to the movies, I am always surprised to see so many people sending and receiving text messages during the film. Why did they come to the movies? They apparently would be better off seeing the person they are sending the SMS to. Except that if they were with that person, they would probably be texting someone else. Is it possible to be happy this way? I doubt it. Happiness can be found only in the here and now. Never somewhere else. Never at another time.

Bruno: What bothers you the most when you are communicating with a group of Hearing people?
Rebecca: When there are side conversations. These one-on-one conversations rarely deal with the topic the group is talking about at the time. They are either talking about something which happened to them before or something they will do after. Not about what's going on at the time.
Bruno: At work, most Hearing people frown upon side conversations during meetings, but they all do it.
Rebecca: When it happens to me, I simply say to people: "If you have something private to discuss, then please find a private place to do it." This is a Deaf rule. Because of the visual nature of our language, any side conversations which occur within a group can be "listened" to by everybody. Consequently, they can't be considered as private.

Your body can only be here and now. So should it be with your mind. You cannot change the past, so why would you worry about it? And the only way to change the future is in the present, not the future. This is the secret of powerful communication and of strong human connections: to have both body and mind fully in the here and now when you communicate.

Deaf Tip n°8: Focus on the right thing
Exercises

- Teaching others is the best way to learn. Share something you have learned in this chapter with at least three friends, colleagues, or members of your family.
- For a week, decide every morning what will be the one most important thing – just one – you will focus on during that day. Then, review your commitment in the evening before going to bed.
- What are the topics you have a hard time focusing on? What could you do to stimulate more pleasure or interest in that topic in order to focus more easily on it?
- Who are the people you have a hard time focusing on? What could you do to develop more love or respect for those people, to improve your concentration?
- Postpone your judgment on how people look, how they are dressed, how they behave, the words they use or the accent they have, and listen to them carefully.
- Which conversations trigger discomfort or anger in you? What beliefs or values do you think are challenged by these discussions? How can you put these beliefs and values aside for a few minutes in order to really listen to and understand the other person's point of view?
- What are the most recurrent noises in your environment which interfere with communication? A clock ticking, a noisy fridge, a TV constantly turned on… a noisy colleague or child? Take a few minutes to make a complete list of all the unnecessary noises you have in your professional, social, and private lives. What can you do to stop, or reduce these noises?
- Take the habit of turning your phone off when you are in a meeting, or when you are talking to someone, and next time you go out with someone you love, leave your phone at home or in the car.
- Monitor the verbs you use for a full week. Which tense do you use the most: the past, the present, or the future?
- Try to talk for a full hour using only the present tense.
- How often do you use the sentence: "That's not what you said!"? Replace it with the question: "What did you mean?"
- What could you do to improve your communication with the three people you selected in the introduction?
- Practice, practice, practice.
- Once done, move on to another chapter.

Personal Notes

. . . .

. . . .

. . . .

. . . .

. . . .

. . . .

. . . .

. . . .

. . . .

. . . .

. . . .

. . . .

. . . .

*A picture shows me at a glance
what it takes dozens of pages of a book to expound.
Ivan Turgenev, Russian Writer*

Deaf Tip n°9
Do you see what I say?

Images have a strong impact on people, stronger than words. To prepare Germans for war, the Nazis became experts in using visual aids. They first invested huge sums of money in posters and leaflets before finally understanding that the best visual support for their propaganda was Hitler's body language, the way he used hand gestures and facial expressions to mesmerize the masses.

Hitler was a master of this art, as was Kennedy, even if it was in a completely different way. During the 1960 presidential campaign, the debates between Nixon and Kennedy were broadcasted on radio and on TV at the same time. People who listened to the radio were convinced that Nixon had won the debate and would be the next president. But surprisingly, people who saw the debate on television had no doubt that it would be Kennedy. One debate, two conclusions. How could this be? Because Nixon used words, and Kennedy images. Nixon was wearing a grey suit, had refused to put on makeup, and was not clean-shaven. Kennedy was wearing a black suit, and, having just returned from campaigning in California, had a beautiful tan. Nixon looked uncomfortable in his chair. Kennedy looked confident, dynamic, and healthy.[106] Kennedy won, because, like many other great speakers, he understood that his body was his best ally to convince people of his message.

Images are useful for selling ideas, from a pair of jeans to a can of soda. A friend of mine lived for several weeks with a family in a small, remote village in Senegal. She wanted to live like the local people, away from the comfort and opulence of the West. When she came back, I asked her what she had learned from her experience. Her answer was surprising. She explained that when she arrived, the whole village celebrated her arrival with a special dish: white rice with a green sauce. On the next day, the meal was just white rice. No sauce. And so it was on the next day. And the next. And the next. And the next. She said that she — meaning her head, not her body — felt hungry for the first week, but after ten days of such a dull diet, she started to eat to live, instead of living to eat. She discovered that she could easily function for a full day, with just a bowl of rice, without feeling hungry. The main lesson she learned in Senegal was that in the West, we don't eat because we are hungry, we eat because we are constantly visually stimulated: when we open the fridge, turn on the TV, or read a magazine. We don't gain weight because we can't resist food. We gain weight because we can't resist visual stimuli.

Use your body

Sign Language has the advantage of being physical, and consequently visible. The result is that more can be expressed with a sign than with a word. Let's start with the basics. If you are a Hearing person, are you able to pronounce two or three letters at the same time? No? In Sign Language you can. I am sure you have already seen the famous *I Love You* sign, which is a combination of the letters I + L + Y:

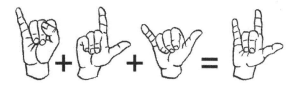

But do you know how to ask where the restrooms are? In French Sign Language, no need to use endless sentences, which is an advantage when you are in a hurry. Two letters W + C (Water Closet) combined into one sign will do:

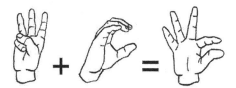

So it is with words. Can you pronounce your name and surname at the same time? No? Deaf people can. They can spell their name with one hand, and simultaneously their surname with the other. When Hearing people invite you for a drink, what information do you capture, except that they are inviting you for a drink? Using their whole body to communicate, when Deaf people invite you for a drink, you can see where it will take place, what you will be drinking, what the atmosphere will be like, how long it will last, and what is the required dress code. Useful information to avoid any unpleasant surprises.

When Deaf people talk about Hearing people, they often describe them as stone statues, referring to their low level of physical expression. When Hearing people observe Deaf people communicating, they can't refrain from thinking that they – Hearing people – underuse their most precious ally to transmit messages, to influence and convince: their body.

It is only when Hearing people want to make sure that they will be understood, that, suddenly, their bodies come alive, moving from a dimensionless language to a 3-D language, like Sign Language. In aviation, for example, in order to save as many lives as possible in an emergency situation, safety procedures are described not only on cards, and orally through the aircraft sound system, but more importantly, through miming by the cabin crew. An approach which would be even more efficient if passengers were requested to imitate at the same time the body movements made by the cabin crew. We all turn into cabin attendants when we try to guide a friend on the phone who is lost, or when we attempt to explain to someone where we have put something. Whenever someone does not understand what we say, our hands, our face, and the rest of our body suddenly start talking. Everybody does it. Even blind people. Why? Why do we move our hands when other people, or even ourselves, can't see them? Because we use our body not only to help other people understand us better, but also to help ourselves.

When you don't remember a word, don't you, unconsciously, watch your hands describing it? When you do, instantly, the word comes back to your mind. Let's say you forgot the word *sharpen*? Sharpen your left index with your right index as if you were sharpening a knife, and as if by magic, the word will come back to you.[107] Words are imprinted in your brain, as much as in your body, and the two are tightly linked together. That's what a team of researchers at the University of Chicago discovered when monitoring children over four years, finding that the more children used their bodies to talk (e.g., moving the head right and left when saying no), the faster they integrated vocabulary.[108] Our body helps us remember words. It helps us select them more appropriately. It helps us and others understand what we say. It forces people to pay more attention to our message, and it helps them remember it.

Oliver: When I was twenty, I went to a summer camp with a group of Deaf children. All day long we did our best to tire them out so they would sleep at night.
Bruno: And what did you do in the evenings?
Oliver: Well, as we were in the middle of nowhere, I transformed myself into a TV screen every night.

Bruno: Into a TV screen???

Oliver: [laugh] Yes. One night I asked them if they had seen Indiana Jones. They had. So I asked them if they wanted to see one of his adventures. They all smiled and sat down quietly. I gave them a short summary of the Raiders of the Lost Ark, the Temple of Doom, and the Last Crusade, and asked them which one they wanted to see. They selected the Last Crusade.

Bruno: You're a regular DVD rental kiosk!

Oliver: [laugh] I first started to describe the main characters, their faces, clothing, personalities, and roles. I described Henry Jones Sr. the scholarly archeologist in his tweed suit, his friend, the museum owner Marcus Brody, the greedy and wealthy businessman, Walter Donovan, who wants eternal life, the beautiful but perfidious Elsa Schneider who works for the Nazis, Sallah the big and friendly Egyptian excavator, and of course Indiana Jones Junior, with his bullwhip and pistol attached to his belt, his leather flight jacket, his sweaty kaki shirt, his unshaven face with a scar on his chin, and his deep blue eyes looking at you from under the shade of his fedora. At that point, I was no longer Olivier for them, I was Indiana Jones. Then, I started the movie. I acted out the kidnapping of Henry Jones while he was searching for the Holy Grail, the diary he left behind, Indiana and Marcus travelling to Venice, Indiana face to face with Hitler, the Joneses escaping Nazi Germany in a Zeppelin, then on a biplane, Henry Jones accidentally shooting down their own plane, their miraculous survival from the crash, and the Joneses ambushing a convoy of Nazi tanks to rescue Marcus. There was not a peep. The kids were all captivated, their eyes and mouths wide open… A bit like you now [laughs again].

Bruno: Ooops. Sorry.

Oliver: [Smile] I went on with Donovan shooting Indiana's father to force him to get the Holy Grail. You could see the fear on the children's faces. Indiana succeeding his way through the three trials of God. Donovan drinking from the wrong cup and turning into dust. Indiana saving his father. Elsa dying in the collapse of the temple. Marcus and the Joneses returning home, leaving behind them a cloud of dust and ashes. The kids were laughing and shouting to express their joy.

Bruno: Wow!

Oliver: [Smile again] Yes. They were all glued to the TV screen: me. Then, they went to bed, quietly, to dream of their hero. Indiana Jones remained in the kids' conversations throughout the rest of the camp.

If you are a Hearing person, all your life you have been trained to freeze every muscle in your body: "Don't point with your finger," "Stand still," "Sit straight," "Close your mouth," "Don't make faces," and now, science tells you that a conscious, clear, and active body language helps improve your memory,[109] your communication with others, and that if you use expressive body language, others consider you warmer, more energetic, and more trustworthy. Does this mean that we all should turn into mimes, cabin attendants, or human TVs? Of course not. But maybe we should make an effort to use our body more to support and clarify our thoughts and our words. A colleague of mine has the habit of excusing himself when he makes a mistake and wiping an imaginary blackboard separating us. Through this simple body movement, he stops people from focusing on his mistake, helps them erase the wrong information in their minds, and gets their brain ready for the new data. Here are additional ways to communicate in a much more visual manner.

Use visual supports

One evening when my youngest son was barely six, as my wife was picking him up from school, his teacher took her aside for a chat.
"Does your husband work for the army?" she asked.
"No. Why?"
"Oh, he doesn't? Then, *you* work for the army, right?"
"No, I don't either. Why makes you think that?"
Taking a piece of paper from her pocket and placing it in front of my wife's eyes she said:
"Did you know that your child is able to list more than twenty weapons?"
And indeed, on the piece of paper there were twenty weapons written in a child's handwriting. Most surprisingly, the weapons were not the basic *bow* and *gun* which kids often refer to at that age, but sophisticated weapons such as the Walther P99 semi-automatic pistol, or the AK74 assault rifle. My wife called me to share her concern and I came home early. We asked Liam:
"Your teacher told us that you are able to list 20 different weapons. Where did you learn that?"
"I invented them" was his sincere reply.

I found interesting that such specific data could enter the brain of a child without his being able to track down its origin. During the following days, we kept a careful eye on Liam, until one day we found him quietly sitting in the corner of a room, listening to his big brother playing a James Bond video game with a friend. One was shouting to the other: "Take a grenade!!! Take a grenade!!!"

Trying to teach your child a poem or the multiplication tables without the support of visual aids will take hours. Put your kid in front of a video game and he or she will remember everything in just a few minutes. Children need visual supports to learn fast. And so do we. Whatever the age of the person you are talking to, he will always pay more attention to you and to what you say if you use visuals. And to get the right visuals, you don't need a lot of money, just a little creativity.

One day I went to one of the most boring conferences I have ever been to. One guy sitting next to me was sleeping so comfortably that he was snoring. The third speaker was talking, and his words were like a sleeping pill. I quickly looked at the program and was horrified to see that there were still five speakers left. As I was lost in my thoughts, the next speaker stood up. It was a young man who was fairly unknown. He stood up and remained silent in front of the audience until everyone had woken up and looked at him. Then, he took off his right shoe, placed it on the podium, and started his talk. I looked at the audience and saw that everyone was focused. The talk wasn't great, but people were focused. Once done, the speaker started to walk away from the podium with only one shoe on. Then, he stopped. People were alert, waiting for an explanation as to why he had placed the other shoe there. He turned around, picked up his shoe, and, approaching the microphone, said: "Oh. Maybe you are wondering why I put my right shoe here? Well, I just wanted you to pay attention to my speech. And you did. Thank you." There was a burst of laughter and a round of applause.

Of course, I would not recommend using this young man as a model. Visual aids should always support a message, never replace or distract from it. However, this anecdote clearly shows how visual aids can captivate people's attention and how, consequently, they can improve communication. The difficulty remains, however, in finding the right visual support, and in reaching the right balance between show and tell.

Lew: I really understood how important visual supports were when I was in high school.
Bruno: Why? What happened?
Lew: I always had so many problems lip-reading the teachers who only talked. But those who used visual aids such as a sketch on the blackboard, a color picture or the object they were describing (a giant molecule, a skeleton, etc.), be it in mathematics, biology, economics, or language courses, I would suddenly be able to read their lips!
Bruno: And how do you think we can apply this principle to our daily lives?
Lew: Easy. Always write down any key information you give to someone, like a phone number. Everybody should do this. Deaf people as well as Hearing people.[110]

To do this, always have a notebook, post-its, or a piece of paper and a pen with you. Don't use them to take notes about what people say, but to illustrate what you say to people. Giving directions to someone? Draw a map. Describing the layout of your house? Draw a sketch. Don't have a piece of paper? Use the wall,[111] the palm of your hand, or simply use the air as canvas. And if you are having lunch, use the table cloth, or the silverware. It is amazing what you can represent with knives, forks, spoons, and a few breadcrumbs!

Use visual words

Once you are able to use your body better and find the right visual aids, you should add to your skills the use of visual words: the ability to talk in such a way that images naturally pop up in the brains of people who are listening to you. To do this, you must first have a clear picture in your mind of what you wish to say. If you don't see it yourself, how do you expect others to visualize it?

Not long ago, I had the chance to take part in an incredible experiment. The exercise was conducted by an actor. After an hour of warm up activities, he asked us – there were about ten participants – to walk around the room for a few minutes, silently, with an imaginary animal. The results were stunning. When people were really into it, convinced that they were walking an elephant, a tiger, or a gold fish, everyone could see the elephant, the tiger, or the gold fish! But when participants could not imagine that they were walking around with a *real* animal, then, the others could only see someone walking around with their arm at 45°. Nothing else. The clearer an image is in your mind, the more visual the words you use to describe it will be, and, accordingly, the more people will see what you see.

Even Sign Language can be more or less visual. The usual sign in French Sign Language for *vacation* is made by crossing the arms on the chest, and lightly tapping the index and middle finger of each hand on the shoulders. But there is another way to say it which I prefer. It consists of opening the upper part of your skull with one hand, like you would open a teapot, taking your brain out with the other hand, and placing it carefully on a table nearby. It represents exactly what I want to do when I am on vacation.

What Deaf people do with their hands, Hearing people do with their words. It is possible to talk like Deaf people sign. It just requires some creativity and a lot of practice. For example:

Instead of saying …	… You could say
I am stressed out	My stomach is full of knots
I took a chance on	I rolled the dice
She is always happy	She is a sunbeam
I like to hear that	It's music to my ears
He has charisma	He's a rock star
She destroys everything	She's a tsunami
He is cold with people	He is a block of ice
There are ups and downs	Life is a roller coaster

Did you notice how, in your inner eye, you automatically saw words in the first case, and images in the second? This is good, specifically if the image is strongly linked to the message you wish to send. This is why metaphors are more useful than idiomatic expressions. When you use the idiomatic expressions *take the cake* or *stop the clock*, they might create images in the mind of the people who are listening to you, but they don't give them a clue as to what you are talking about. In this case, being visual becomes counterproductive. The objective of being visual is to help other people visualize what you say, not to confuse them more.

Use stories

I was raised in the countryside. I had two brothers, one sister, and many friends who I played with in the surrounding fields. My grandmother also lived with us, and her wisdom was equal to her age. One day, as I was complaining about one of the family rules, seeing only the restriction which was imposed on me, my grandma, who was walking by, stopped, looked at me, and without any preamble, told me the following story:

People came from far away to watch the clowns, the lions, and the horses of that little circus do a thousand tricks. But the highlight of the show was always the tightrope walker. A balancing pole in his hands, he would walk, run, and dance on a tight rope ten meters above the ground without even a safety net. Every evening more and more people came to see him. He knew it and he liked it. To remain the star of the show, every night the tightrope walker would invent new tricks, each one more impressive than the last. One night, as thousands of spectators were sitting in the circus tent admiring him, the tightrope walker thought: Why do I bother with this long pole? I'm the best tightrope walker in the world. This pole is a burden. If I get rid of it, I will be able to perform new tricks, and my fans will love me even more. No sooner said than done. That evening, in front of a record crowd of spectators, the tightrope walker ventured out onto his rope without his pole. After a few steps, he suddenly lost his balance, and without his pole was unable to regain it. In front of the horrified eyes of the spectators, the tightrope walker fell to his death. The balancing pole, which he had seen for so many years as a burden, had in fact saved his life all those years.

My grandma looked me straight in the eyes and then left, leaving me alone with this story and with my thoughts. She didn't scold or reproach me. She just told me a little story which was worth a thousand words. The message was so obvious that I couldn't ignore it. Today, my grandma is gone, but the message is still there. A message which, through a story, is rooted to my life. A message which regularly reminds the rebellious part of me that rules save lives, including mine.

"Most of what we know, or think we know, we have never personally experienced," said Gerbner. "We live in a world erected by the stories we hear and see and tell."[112]

David: Like the stories you find in the oral tradition of most Deaf schools.
Bruno: What stories?
David: Stories about special events, anecdotes about teachers, or incredible achievements by students. In Deaf schools, they are passed down from one year to the next until everyone knows about them as if they had been present, even if those events occurred several decades earlier.
Bruno: How is it done? Through Sign Language?
David: Signs and mime. The way it's done is so precise, the story tellers so accurate and expressive in their narration, reproducing the twitches of the protagonists and every detail of the anecdote, that after a few weeks it's difficult to say if you've heard the story or if you actually witnessed it.
Bruno: ... because of the visual way these stories are told...

David: Exactly. One evening several years after I left school, I entered a pub and immediately recognized a former student from my school. I had never seen him before, yet I immediately knew who he was and everything about his feats. A fascinating experience.[113]

Everyone has heard about Steve Jobs' garage, or about Dr. Pemberton's secret recipe for producing Coca-Cola. Everyone knows the story of Ray Kroc investing his entire life savings into milkshake makers at the age of 52, which quickly led him to meet the McDonald Brothers. Everyone knows how Post-its®, the most successful 3M product, was created out of glue that didn't stick, by a chemist singing in a church choir who was tired of losing his hymnal bookmarks. Everyone has read how the gold banana pin, the highest reward at Foxboro, came about from a scientist, who saved the company in its early days with an invention, and its president who had nothing else in his drawer but a banana to reward him with.

Whether true, partly true, or completely false, these stories are more than foundational. It is through them that the real beliefs and values of a group – a company, a club, a church, a political party, a family, etc. – are transmitted. It is through stories that people know if they fit into a group's culture or not. Stories teach us what is true or false, good or bad. They define the soul of a group and influence the behavior of its members. Anybody can disagree with a belief or a value, but how can you disagree with a story? Stories are powerful because they send us back to the way people communicated at the beginning of humanity. Stories are powerful because they communicate directly with our primitive brain, the amygdala, and produce strong emotions, which are the glue for our memory.

So if you want to promote a value or energize a group, if you want people to remember what you say, or if you don't want to answer a question directly, tell a story. But when you do, make sure that you apply the following basic principles:

First, ask yourself what specific message you want to transmit, and what message your listeners are expecting.[114] Then, select the story, or the anecdote, which is the most appropriate for the message you want to convey, the type of public you have in front of you, and their expectations. Choose a story you enjoy telling. Anecdotes are better if they are personal and true. If you don't believe in what you say, no one else will either. If you don't enjoy telling the story, no one will enjoy listening to it. And please, always follow this simple rule: one lesson, one story. If you want to transmit several messages, then find several stories.

Second, before starting, rearrange the physical setting of the room if you can.[115] Avoid visual and audio distractions. Avoid too much light. Avoid having people sit too far apart or too far from you. I remember a great experience I had with a group of teenagers. I wanted them to share personal anecdotes about the people who had played an important role in their lives. But they were very shy. So we sat in a circle and bent forward, shoulder to shoulder, nearly head to head, as if we were going to share an important secret. Then, I started to talk about the teacher who had influenced me the most. Once I had finished, as if by magic, one after the other, they all shared personal anecdotes which were important to them.

Third, learn your introduction by heart in order to give yourself confidence. There should be no hesitation in your voice or in your choice of words during the first few minutes. Start as if you were gathering your thoughts, recalling an important event from the past. Set the scene. Describe the background. Create atmosphere. Use visual words which will stimulate people' senses. Describe sounds, tastes, touch, scents, shapes, colors, and textures. Then, introduce the main characters. Describe their physical appearance, and their psychological make-up. Like the masks used in ancient Greece to allow spectators to see and understand the emotions of the actors from afar, don't be afraid to caricature a bit the people you are talking about, and the situation. You are not a historian. The purpose is not to describe the truth as objectively as possible. On the contrary, you have to be subjective if you want people to feel what you feel, and see what you see.

Fourth, create suspense as you tell the story. Feel the anticipation of your listeners. Are they waiting for the next sentence? Is your style vibrant and your body language lively? Play with sounds and silences. Use catchwords and recurrent phrases. And remember Deaf Tip n°5: remain simple and precise. The new zapping generation has a short attention span, problems visualizing something they cannot see, and yet, is more demanding.[116]

Fifth, connect with your audience. Observe people. Look them in the eyes.[117] Are they reacting to your story the way you want? Can you see in their body language, and in the sounds they make if they are with you? If not, adapt your style, rhythm, and timing. And once you have finished your story, stop! Don't go back and clarify a part you are not happy with. Your conclusion must be short and sharp. Let people go away thinking about the lesson, about how it relates to their own life. If there is applause or laughter at the end, great, but if your audience remains completely silent, don't necessarily conclude that you failed. Silence can be an even greater sign of success. Sometimes, people need to savor what they have just heard in silence, meditating on what it means to them.

Once you have incorporated all these recommendations, practice over and over again. Tell tales, stories, and anecdotes to your neighbors' kids. If they survive, do the same with your own kids, and with your partner. And if, after that, you are still welcome in your house, then tell them to your friends, colleagues, and clients. Practicing will help you develop your own style, and understand which parts of each story you should keep or take out. Remember that the best stories you can tell are always experiences which happened to you, specifically those which made you learn and grow. These are the best because you know them better than anyone else. These are the best because by telling them, they will have a therapeutic effect on you. These are the best because they will help you become conscious of your beliefs, values, patterns, and psychological traps. These are the best because people can't resist the truth. These are the best because you are the stories you tell, and by telling them, people will understand who you are. And the more they understand who you are, the more they will enjoy relating to you.

Deaf Tip n°9: Do you see what I say?
Exercises

- Teaching others is the best way to learn. Share something you have learned in this chapter with at least three friends, colleagues, or members of your family.
- Are people able to read your emotions? For a full month, practice making faces every morning in front of the mirror, expressing different emotions.
- Regularly play mime games with your family and friends. Who are the most gifted? Why? What could you do to become as good as they are?
- Buy a notebook and a pen small enough to fit in your pocket or in your purse. Carry them with you at all times, and when you explain something, use them to draw illustrations.
- For a full week, every morning invent a new metaphor which will trigger in people's inner eye a surprising image or movie, and then use it at least twice during the day.
- Interview people you love – grandfathers and grandmothers are best for this exercise – and ask them to share with you their stories and anecdotes: Who was their most famous ancestor? What is the first national or international event they remember? What is their best memory from school years? What is the most stupid thing they have ever done? What was their best vacation, ever? What was their most memorable birthday, Christmas, or New Year? Who is the teacher they remember the most? Who was their best friend? Who was their first love? How did they meet? What was the happiest day of their life? And the saddest? What is the best joke they have ever played on someone? What is the most terrifying accident they have ever had in their life? And so on. Prepare a long list of questions before starting the interview, break up the interview into several one hour sessions, and encourage them not to answer with short sentences, but to share the whole story with you.
- Recall three experiences in your life where you learned something important which made you grow, and share them with three people.
- What could you do to improve your communication with the three people you selected in the introduction?
- Practice, practice, practice.
- Once done, move on to another chapter.

Personal Notes

. . . .

. . . .

. . . .

. . . .

. . . .

. . . .

. . . .

. . . .

. . . .

. . . .

. . . .

. . . .

. . . .

The only way I can understand a piece of information
is by visualizing it.
Emmanuelle Laborit, French Actress

Deaf Tip n°10
Listen in Technicolor

Some years ago, I heard a strange conversation between my wife and her sister. It was after a good dinner we had had by the swimming pool. They started to talk about *Harry Potter and the Deathly Hallows*. Both had read the book, both had loved the movie, and they were now talking about it excitedly. But soon the conversation turned strange as they started to describe the last ten minutes of the movie. The story was the same, but the way they each pictured it was completely different. As they were debating who had the worst memory, one of our adolescent children sat down with us for a few minutes, listened to the debate, and then left the table with a sarcastic look on his face, saying: "You are talking about a movie you haven't even seen. It hasn't been released yet!" Long silence. The movie was indeed only to be released a few months later. The debate they were having was not, as they had thought, about the movie they had seen at the cinema, but about the one they had seen in their heads while reading the book. No wonder they were different.

It is not the originality of a plot, the richness of the vocabulary, or the sophistication of the syntax which turns a book into a best seller. A book becomes a best seller only when it triggers images in our head, when it prompts a movie on our internal screen, when it immerses us in the action as if we were there. It is images, not words, which trigger emotions in us. It is not the words *angry dog* which scare us, it is the image that the words project on our inner screen, the image of a dog growling, teeth bared, hair and tail raised.

Without images and emotions, we have no memory. Without memory, we have no past. And without a past, we are nobody. When we read a book or listen to people, we can decide to focus either on words or on images.[118] When we read words or listen to people, we forget. When we play the movie of what we read or of what we hear in our mind's eye, we remember. We can listen to people with our left brain. Or we can listen to them with our right brain. It is our choice. It is your choice.

How does it work?

Each hemisphere of the brain plays a different role. Just like our two arms, and our two legs, our two hemispheres are separate and autonomous, each with a specific personality. The Right Hemisphere (RH) is divergent and open to new experiences. The Left Hemisphere (LH) is convergent, logical, and sequential, focusing on detailed tasks. Some experts believe that this double personality developed at the beginning of the human race, when one part of us had to concentrate on step-by-step processes such as sharpening flint, while the other part had to remain on the lookout for any potential danger, like a saber-toothed tiger jumping out from behind a nearby bush. Whatever the origin of this double personality, today nothing has changed. Even if we have traded our leopard skins for pure wool slim fit suits, our LH still focuses on the details of complex tasks such as decrypting e-mails, while our RH vigilantly scans the environment for a manager who might suddenly jump out from behind a nearby cubicle.

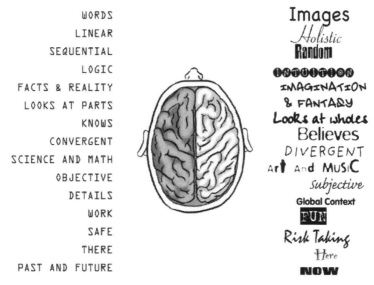

WORDS	Images
LINEAR	Holistic
SEQUENTIAL	Random
LOGIC	
FACTS & REALITY	IMAGINATION
LOOKS AT PARTS	& FANTASY
KNOWS	Looks at wholes
CONVERGENT	Believes
SCIENCE AND MATH	DIVERGENT
OBJECTIVE	Art And MUSiC
DETAILS	subjective
WORK	Global Context
SAFE	FUN
THERE	Risk Taking
PAST AND FUTURE	Here
	NOW

Nothing has changed, except that during the last two centuries, in the name of science and capitalism, western cultures have strongly privileged the LH. Within the family circle, day dreaming, imagination, and fantasy are quickly discouraged. At school, mathematics is presented as the road to success. And in the corporate world, convergence, objectivity, and logic are favored over divergence, subjectivity, and intuition. Not surprisingly, since in a fast changing world, facts and convictions are more reliable than beliefs and fantasy. The West has favored the LH so much that it seems that our RH suffers today from atrophy because of disuse.

It is said that Gordon MacKenzie, the famous designer of Hallmark Cards, often visited schools to share his love for drawing with children. MacKenzie would often start his presentation by telling kids that he was an artist. Then, looking at the class, he would ask: "How many artists do we have in this room?" MacKenzie reports that in kindergarten all the children would raise their hands. In second grade only three-fourths would. And by sixth grade, not one single hand would go up.[119]

LH/RH impact on communication

Oral languages are decrypted in Wernicke's area which is located in the left cerebral hemisphere.[120] This is logical because oral languages are extremely structured (grammar, syntax, conjugation), sequential, and linear (only one sound can be pronounced at a time). But what about Sign languages? As they are purely visual and holistic, like a dance, (hand movements, facial expressions, and body language are all used at the same time), does it mean that Sign languages are rooted in the RH instead of the LH? To check this assumption, scientists have used functional magnetic resonance imaging (fMRI) and have discovered that, as with Hearing people, intense cerebral activity occurs in the LH of Deaf people when they sign. This is an important discovery, as this strong left-lateralized neural activity during Sign Language production shows that language is universal, be it vocal-aural, or visual-manual. However, this is only part of the picture. While Hearing and Deaf people have the same LH neural activity when they express themselves (production), they have different neural activity when they listen to others (reception).

Hearing people   **Deaf people**

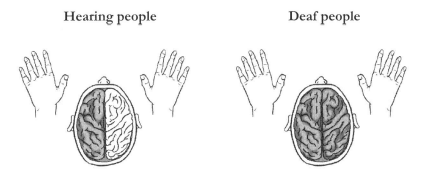

While Hearing people's cerebral activity is mainly limited to the LH when they listen, native signers[121] show an extensive RH activation,[122] in addition to similar LH activity, possibly because Deaf people pay more attention than Hearing people to the other's body movements, faces[123] and emotional expressions,[124] a type of visual decoding which is specific to the RH.

Miguel: I'm not surprised by these discoveries. When I listen, I don't hear words, I see images.

Bruno: What do you mean?

Miguel: It's like an association of images. If someone says "Do you want a glass of water?" I don't see the words *glass* or *water*, I see a glass of water which I associate with the feeling of thirst.

Bruno: So that's how you think?

Miguel: Yes. I never hear voices, nor see words. Not even in my dreams. I either see a movie or hand movements.

Bruno: But don't you sometimes talk in your sleep, like Hearing people do?

Miguel: Sure I do, except that in my case, it's my hands that move.

Listening in images with the RH like Deaf people do is more effective than listening to words with only the LH, like Hearing people do. British writer Daniel Tammet – who has savant syndrome (like that portrayed by Dustin Hoffman in the movie *Rain Man)* and vivid synesthesia – seems to support this idea. Tammet speaks twelve languages, and was able to list publicly in 2004, 22514 decimals of pi in 5 hours and 9 minutes, without making a single mistake. When asked how he could remember so many languages, and play so easily with numbers – a task which is specific to the LH – Tammet's answer was surprising: "I see words and numbers in a three dimensional landscape, with shapes, colors, textures and movement." Tammet describes number *one* as blinding, like a torch in the eyes and number *five* like waves breaking on rocks. The name *Richard* is red and *Henry* is white. The word *dog* looks like three circles broken up by a line, starting at the top of the first circle and finishing at the bottom of the last circle with a curl. Tammet is even able to reproduce words and numbers as he sees them[125] in 3D with modeling clay. Something that only the RH can do.

If this way of thinking is disconcerting for Hearing people, it isn't for Deaf people who wonder if sound is warm, if red is an angry color, or if blue sounds wet.[126] Hearing people see numbers with their LH, as abstract symbols, having no intrinsic meaning – even if initially they were created to help traders keep track of their dealings with each symbol representing a specific sum by the number of its inner angles. In contrast, Deaf people see numbers with their RH. As each number is a mix of finger positions and hand movements, they see numbers as shapes, images, or even objects, with a specific texture and color. The number 20, for example, is made in French Sign Language with the tip of the index finger touching the tip of the thumb twice, the rest of the hand remaining closed. In this case, the LH sees in this sign the number 20, but the RH undoubtedly sees a bird. And people who are able to completely block the LH, are even able to describe with their RH what type of bird, its size, shape, and color.

Let's see how different it is to listen with the RH compared to with the LH. Let's start with the LH. Please look at the following drawings for one minute, and try to remember each of them in association with the number next to them in the same box.

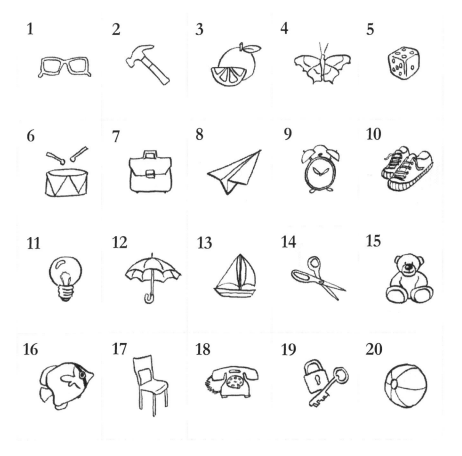

Now, without going back to the previous drawings, try to recall the missing objects and numbers. Of course, the order in the chart has been changed.

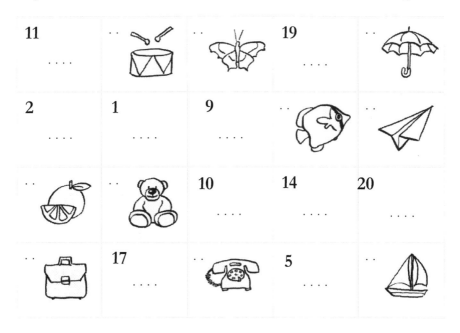

How many pairs were you able to remember correctly? Write your result in the box below.

Hearing people are able to remember six pairs (object + number) on average – often the three first and the three last in the chart – while Deaf people are able to remember a minimum of fourteen pairs. Why such a difference? Because when doing this exercise, Hearing people naturally use their LH to remember the numbers and the RH to remember the images, while Deaf people use their RH for both numbers and images. By storing information in the same half of the brain (RH+RH instead of LH+RH) and by using images and emotions, Deaf people naturally increase their ability to remember. I've conducted this exercise a hundred times, pitting Hearing and Deaf people against each other from all over the world: Europe, North America, and the Middle East, and the results have always been the same. Without fail, Deaf people always beat Hearing people.

Then, one day I was invited to China to deliver a course on communication with Deaf facilitators. To do so, I made contact with a Deaf association in Beijing, and arrived a day early before the start of the course to brief my three new Deaf colleagues on the different exercises we would be doing. On the following day I entered the training room, confident that the trainees would experience and learn the same things as people from other cultures. To my astonishment, I saw for the first time Hearing people who could remember more than 16 pairs, beating Deaf people in this memory exercise! I was speechless. My belief that Deaf people had better memories because of their over trained RH was shaken. As I was sharing with the Chinese trainees my surprise, explaining how this usually worked in other countries, a participant stood up, went to the paperboard, drew an umbrella, and then asked me: "What do you call this?" Without understanding where he wanted to go, I wrote on the left side of his drawing the English word: *Umbrella*. Then, he asked: "What is the correlation between what I drew and what you wrote?" "None," I said. "The correlation is just based on a social convention." He went on: "Do you know how we write *umbrella* in Chinese?" He carefully calligraphed on the right side of the drawing the following pictogram:

Then, he looked at me with a big smile, and said: "Do you understand? Chinese people listen like Deaf people, with the right brain!" I started to understand. As we were still discussing what was a new discovery for me, another participant came in with a stack of cards with ancient Chinese pictograms. In no more than one minute, he showed me thirty different pictograms, and explained their meanings to me (some of the simplest examples are given in the chart below). Then, he reshuffled the cards, and showed them to me again, one after the other, asking me what they meant. To my own surprise, I could remember every single Chinese sign without any mistakes.

English	Human	Rain	Mountain	Fish	Sun
Chinese					

Of course, Chinese pictograms have evolved, becoming more and more abstract over time. Nevertheless, to the expert eye, the origin of each pictogram is still visible. For example, take the character 大 which represents a man of great stature and means *big*. If you now want to write *husband*, just add a little stroke on the top of the pictogram to represent the clip that the ancient Chinese wore at the age of 20 to keep their hair in place to show people that they had reached adulthood and could marry. Below, the evolution of the pictogram:

Like signs, Chinese pictograms don't represent words. A pictogram, like a sign, can convey an idea, or an entire sentence. Like signs, pictograms are more like images, art, or music (RH), than words, and mathematics (LH). But is it sufficient to conclude, as my trainee suggested, that Chinese people listen like Deaf people with both hemispheres? Indeed, maybe. Recently, scientists have demonstrated that if Westerners have such a hard time learning Mandarin, it is because they listen with their right ear (controlled by the LH), trying to decrypt a code (LH), instead of listening with their left ear (controlled by the RH) enjoying a new type of music with a wide range of tones (RH).[127]

What would happen if, like Deaf people, you listened with your RH? To find out, prepare yourself by transferring numbers from your LH to your RH. Do this by counting from 1 to 20, linking each number with a hand movement representing an object. Look at your hands when you do it. Do it several times, until all three (the number, the hand movement, and the object) are strongly linked, and come to your mind automatically without any effort. The objects described below are only suggestions; you can create your own if you wish to.

01	One hand closed, thumb up, placed on the back of the other hand which is flat. You visualize the first step of a **podium**.
02	Index finger horizontal, thumb vertical, and the other fingers closed. Looking at the two fingers you see a **gun**.
03	The middle finger and the index finger are a **dolphin**. The thumb up is its dorsal fin. The hand moves like a wave.
04	Four fingers opened and stretched out pointing to the sky. You see the crown of the **Statue of Liberty**.
05	The five fingers of one hand are positioned in the shape of a C and hold an imaginary **glass of water**.
06	One hand closed, thumb up. The other hand palm side down, in a cup shape, on top of the thumb. You see a **mushroom**.
07	One hand palm down. It's the sea. The other hand is closed, index finger horizontal representing a **submarine**, thumb up like a periscope.
08	Each hand has four fingers open. A quick sharp movement represents bear claws.
09	Five fingers open represent the lawn. Four fingers of the other hand scrape the lawn like a **rake**.
10	Pulling up your **socks** with the index and thumb of each hand, all the other fingers open, ten in total.
11	Pushing with the two thumbs – all the other fingers closed – the last piece of a **jigsaw puzzle**.
12	A **nail** represented by a thumb, being pulled by the thumb and index of the other hand.
13	A thumb up, the other thumb, index and middle fingers vibrating on top of the first thumb, like the rotor of a **helicopter**.
14	One index represents someone. The four fingers open, thumb closed, of the other hand move as a hand **fan**.
15	A **policeman** (representing ten) makes the stop sign with the right hand, the five fingers open.
16	The right thumb goes from the mouth to the envelope made with the other hand, to glue a **stamp**.
17	Five fingers hold a **potato**. The thumb and index of the other hand, slightly crooked, use a peeler.
18	One arm vertical with the hand open. Three fingers of the other hand hit it, making a **spot**.
19	One arm vertical, hand and fingers opened in a tree. The four other fingers move down in a pendulum movement. It is a falling **leaf**.
20	A **bird**. The thumb and index finger are touching quickly their tips, like the beak of a bird.

When you are able to count to 20, connecting each number to a hand movement and to the corresponding object, you are ready to listen with your RH. Now, do the exercise again, this time like a Deaf person.

Use each hand movement as a bridge between your LH which stores numbers and your RH which records objects. Do this by playing twenty short video clips on your mind's screen. For example, if you want to link number 1 to an umbrella, and if you have decided that 1 is made with your hand closed, one thumb up placed on the back of the other hand to represent the first step of a podium, then, make this hand movement, look at it, and play on your mind's screen a short video linking an umbrella with the first step of a podium.[128] Don't hesitate to add emotions as it will help you fix the video in your memory. For example, Mary Poppins and her famous umbrella could land on the first step of a podium during the 1936 Berlin Olympics. To link number 2 to a ball, look at your two fingers representing number two as well as a gun, and visualize a gun shooting a ball. Once again, try to stimulate as much as possible the emotions you feel as you play the video clip in your mind. In this last example, you could visualize the ball exploding into a thousand pieces. Now, do the same with the other associations:

01 + Umbrella
02 + Ball
03 + Alarm clock
04 + Butterfly
05 + Orange
06 + Teddy bear
07 + Suitcase
08 + Light bulb
09 + Hammer
10 + Boat
11 + Scissors
12 + Glasses
13 + Dice
14 + Drums
15 + Tennis shoes
16 + Paper plane
17 + Key
18 + Phone
19 + Fish
20 + Chair

If you did it right, you should now have twenty short video clips stored in your brain. Next, hide the list above, take a pen, and complete the chart on the next page with either the number or the missing object. To help you retrieve the appropriate video clip, once again use your hands. If you are looking for an object, make the hand movement of the corresponding number in the chart. What object does it represent, and when you see it, what is the other object which suddenly appears? If you are looking for a number, project in your mind's eye the object which you find in the chart. What other object appears with it? To which hand movement, and consequently to which number, does it correspond?

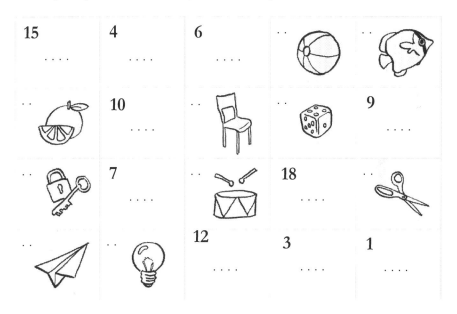

Compare your results with the previous one. Surprising, isn't it? Hearing people see the world as a book, Deaf people as a movie. Hearing people think in words, Deaf people in images. If you want to listen and remember, then, like Deaf people, listen in Technicolor. Send your LH on vacation, and listen with your eyes. Both your physical and your mental eyes. Play a movie in your head when people talk and you will remember what they say.

Listen with your right brain

Even if we have been raised in a strongly LH privileged environment, our primal brain remains the RH. We first started to think and communicate in images, not in words. And this form of communication is still deeply ingrained in us. When you go to a buffet restaurant, even if each dish is described in detail on a little card, you still have to open the lid to see what's inside. And it is what you see, not what you read, which prompts your choice. When you want to buy a car, an apartment, or a house, do you look at the description first, or at the picture? We all look at the picture first. It is only when we like the picture that we take the time to investigate further, and read the description. From our earliest years, we use our RH to record, even if it is unconsciously. We create a mental map when we want to remember a route: right at the post office, left at the big oak tree. We do the same thing when we meet new people, and don't have a piece of paper and a pen on which to discreetly write their name. His name is Paul? Then, I visualize the face of my best friend, whose name is Paul, and merge the two faces together. His family name is Kapp? In this case, I visualize my friend Paul with the cap of my favorite baseball team on his head. And when I see that person again, the face of my friend with a cap naturally appears in my mind's eye, and I remember that his name Paul and his surname Kapp. We do the same thing when we try to follow someone else's logic. A friend of yours talks about the second wife of the brother of his step mother's sister. The only way to understand who your friend is talking about is to do exactly what you have just done when reading this sentence: to quickly draw a family tree in your mind. It is the same in sports. Before a penalty shootout in soccer, a free throw in basketball, or a match point serve in tennis, to improve performance, athletes always visualize in their mind the perfect move, over and over again. A rehearsal which is done by the RH.

The best story I have ever heard on the power of visualization in sports was in diving. Six months before the 2000 Olympics in Sydney, the American 10 meter platform diver Laura Wilkinson broke a bone in her foot during practice. At first, the doctor did not correctly diagnose the injury, and when Laura went to see another doctor five days later, the x-rays revealed that the damaged bones had started to heal incorrectly and it was already too late to put the bones back into the right place. With a broken foot, Laura would no longer have been able to participate in the Olympics. However, despite the situation, her coach didn't give up, and prepared a special training program adapted to her situation. She decided to give it a try. For five months, she put on her swimming suit and climbed the 10 meter platform with a cast on her foot. There she sat, on the edge of the platform, day after day, for hours, visualizing the perfect dive. Three weeks before the competition, the cast was taken off, and she went to the Olympics being the least prepared competitor according to traditional training methods. Starting from 8th place, behind the over-trained Chinese athletes – the overwhelming favorites in this event – Laura had little chance of winning a medal. But against all odds, she reached the final round of dives, beat the flawless Chinese divers, and won the gold medal.[129]

If you are not an Olympic Gold medalist, if you don't have savant syndrome, and if you are not Deaf, where should you start? First, by better using your brain space. We speak about 125 words per minute, while our brain is able to deal on average with 800.[130] This difference means that during any type of conversation, our brain is underused.[131] This is why, when people talk, we are often busy preparing our answer, guessing what they are going to say, or letting our thoughts loose, thinking about other things. And there are of course better ways of using our brain during a conversation. For example, by creating video clips –like we just did in the previous exercise – to remember what people say.

There is no agreed upon definition of what active listening is, even if most descriptions contain these four elements: (1) a structured approach to focusing on what the other person says, (2) postponing judgment, (3) avoiding parallel mental activities, (4) in order to better understand, connect, and collaborate. My definition is much simpler: "Active listening is to see in our mind's eye what others see on theirs." And to achieve this goal, of course, a specific skill – more than just listening – must be developed: the ability to ask questions[132] in order to tape the right video. If a friend tells you: "I went for a walk in the woods." What do you see? What do you tape? If there are woods near your house, you will naturally visualize in your mind's eye your friend walking in those woods. But in reality, your friend prefers walking in *The Woods*, a Mall nearby her house.

When people talk, and when we want to record the right video, we must ask them questions: When? Where? How? until we are able, just like a film director, to see the background, the characters, their personalities and moods, the atmosphere, and hear the dialogue in detail. When questioning is done correctly and when it is done with the right intentions,[133] several positive outcomes emerge. The number of misunderstandings is reduced. People get excited and are willing to open up more. Memory increases. And, having received recognition, people are revitalized with energy, and are now ready to listen (back) to you, as actively as you listened to them.

I have not kept up many contacts with friends from school or university. In fact, I am only still in contact with one friend whose name is Fred. And I have often wondered: Why? Why him? Here is the reason why I believe we are still connected. I met my wife when I was 22. At the time I was in university and I still had three years to go before graduation. I was not rich. I had a pair of jeans, a t-shirt, a place to sleep, and enough money to pay tuition. My only real possession was my motorcycle. When Magali and I decided to get married, I sold my motorcycle to buy the wedding rings.

One year later, on a cold and dark winter night, someone knocked at the door of our apartment. I answered.

"Fred! what are you doing here?"
"Bruno! You have to come with me. I have something to show you!"
"Fred, it's nearly midnight. I can't come with you. I'm married. I don't want to fool around."
"Come on! You won't regret it! I'm telling you – you have to come!"
"Fred, I want to do well in my studies. And for that, I need to sleep."

As if he was not listening to me, Fred kept on insisting, until I finally gave in. I told my wife that I would come back as soon as possible, and I left with him. As we drove out of the city, I repeatedly asked:
"Fred, where are we going?"
"You'll see, you'll see," was always his reply.

We got on the highway and drove for about two hours. It was close to 2 AM, we were in the countryside, and there was not a single house or light which could be seen. I started to get nervous.

"Fred, what crazy plan is this again?"[134]
"Be patient. We are getting close," was his answer.

A few minutes later, he stopped the car in front of a huge building. A man had built in the middle of nowhere the biggest motorcycle shop in Europe - several thousand square meters. The parking lot was not yet finished, but it was possible to walk by the windows and look at hundreds of bikes which came from all over the world: Japan, the UK, Italy, the USA, Canada, Spain, Germany, France, and India. We walked silently along, and looked at all those beautiful machines. Then, we went back to the car, and Fred drove me back to my apartment. I was in bed by 5 AM, dead tired, but so happy. Happy to have seen so many motorcycles, certainly, but even happier to have discovered Fred, it seems, for the first time. I don't know if my family, or even my wife, ever understood how much of a sacrifice it had been for me to sell my bike. But apparently Fred had seen it. He listened to me with his eyes. He recorded the movie on his inner screen. And when he heard about this shop, he didn't just write the address on a piece of paper. No. He came to my apartment, picked me up, and drove me to the place.

Without any doubt, one of the greatest gifts we can offer people is to give them back a movie of an important moment in their life that we have recorded in our mind's eye. This is one of the most beautiful proofs of love. And this is what, I believe, connects me to Fred.

Recording a movie of someone in your mind's eye can be done with anyone: at work, in your social life, and in your family. Your 6 year old son comes back from school all excited:

"Mom! Mom! Moooom!!!"

The tone of the voice and the body language inform you that you should peel your eyes away from your computer, your book, or your pan, stop listening to his words with your LH, and start listening with your eyes and your RH, in order to record a movie in your mind. Look your son straight in the eyes[135] and this gives him the green light to tell you his story.

"Mom, I was in the playground, and there was that little girl crying. There were kids making fun of her. So with my friends we pushed away those kids to defend her…"

As you ask questions to get the details, your son perceives your interest and gets even more excited. As he talks, you play the movie on your internal screen. You see the playground. You see the little girl crying. You see how she is dressed. You see how she is hurt. You see your son running to defend her, like a knight. You have captured the movie. Well done. But you cannot keep it for yourself. It is not yours. It doesn't belong to you. A few hours later, as you are eating altogether at the dinner table, you tell your spouse, in front of your son:

"Honey, do you know what happened to Nick this morning? There was that little girl crying…"

As you start replaying the video, observe your son. Do you see his back straighten up? Do you see his eyes sparkling? Do you see his smile getting bigger? Now, don't tell the whole story. Remember, it is not yours. Let him finish.

"Go on, Nick! Tell Dad what happened."

You won't have to ask him twice.[136] There is even a good chance that the story will get a bit bigger than the one you heard earlier... which was already bigger than what really happened. But who cares. We're not talking about reality here, we're talking about love.

When we listen to words, we forget. When we see images and feel emotions, we remember. Listening in Technicolor improves our memory. And that is not all. It also brings people closer, for the only way for two people to really connect is when both of them see at the same time, on their internal screens, the exact same movie, with the same background, the same colors, the same characters, the same dialogue, and consequently share the same emotions.

Post-Script

As I am working on the conclusion to this chapter, I can hear Magali in the kitchen helping our youngest son learn his geography lesson. Yesterday she tried, unsuccessfully, for two hours to teach him all the capitals of Central and South America. But tonight, something is different. She proofread this chapter this morning and it seems that she is trying a new approach. For each country and for each capital, she is now making drawings on a piece of paper, linking words, sounds, and images together. Argentina becomes a pile of money,[137] Buenos Aires, a window with a fresh breeze coming in,[138] connected together, Liam, on his inner screen, opens a window to see a pile of money. I have a hard time focusing on my writing. I want to know if it will work. I listen carefully. Will I hear sighs and complaining like last night? No. The atmosphere is completely different. Liam is excited, giggling and laughing. Yesterday, after two hours of torture, he couldn't remember any country or capital, and went to bed crying. Tonight, after half an hour of fun, he knows all the countries of Central and South America, and all their capitals!

Deaf Tip n°10: Listen in Technicolor
Exercises

- Teaching others is the best way to learn. Share something you have learned in this chapter with at least three friends, colleagues, or members of your family.
- Observe what happens in your mind's eye when you read a book. What do you see? Words or images?
- Think about two books you have read. Which one do you prefer? Is it because one triggered in your mind's eye a clearer movie than the other one?
- What happens in your mind's eye when you listen to people? When and with whom do you hear words? When and with whom do you see movies? Why?
- The next time that you feel someone wishes to say something important, focus on that person, and ask all the questions you need to in order to reproduce his or her movie on your inner screen.
- Select a few people you love or respect, and recall a movie you have recorded on your inner screen during an important moment of their life. Then, when you feel that the moment is right, show the movie back to them.
- Play a movie on your inner screen of yourself doing something perfectly before a challenging event: speaking with confidence in front of a big audience, brilliantly negotiating an important contract… doing the dishes without breaking a plate, etc.
- Select a behavior or a habit you would like to change (e.g., being aggressive) and create a movie in which you behave as you would like to (e.g., being firm but kind). Play that movie on a regular basis in your mind's eye, specifically before entering into risky situations or meeting people.
- What could you do to improve your communication with the three people you selected in the introduction?
- Practice, practice, practice.
- Once done, move on to another chapter.

Personal Notes

. . . .

. . . .

. . . .

. . . .

. . . .

. . . .

. . . .

. . . .

. . . .

. . . .

. . . .

. . . .

. . . .

The way towards each other is through our bodies.
Words are the longest distance you can travel,
so complex and hazardous you lose your direction.
Jeni Couzyn, South African Psychotherapist and Poet

Deaf Tip n°11
Get in touch

Our skin is by far our largest organ. If we could take it off and lay it flat on a table, it would measure about two square meters, weigh 16% of our body weight, and have a thickness of 0.5 mm (eye lids) to 4 mm (soles of feet). Our skin plays the role of a physical and psychological barrier between ourselves and the external world, a shield between what is inside and what is outside us. It separates us from the world, yet connects us to it at the same time. For example, when we touch something, we are at the same time touched by it. Our skin contains pressure sensors which allow us to pick up objects without dropping or crushing them. It is equipped with pain sensors to avoid unnecessary pain. It is packed with oil glands to keep it smooth and soft, and with sweat glands and hair follicles to regulate the temperature of our body, to cool it down when it is too hot, and to warm it up when it is too cold. Equipped with millions of sensory cells, our skin loves to be touched, rubbed, and caressed. And contrary to our other senses, our sense of touch cannot be turned off. We can close our eyes, plug up our nose, shut our mouth, and block our ears, but we cannot stop getting information through our skin. We could live without eyes, ears, and a tongue, but we could not live without our skin.[139]

A vital need

We all need to be touched in order to feel alive. One evening as I was putting our second son to bed, he asked me: "Dad, can you please lay down on me?" I was surprised by the request but complied, being careful to not crush him. After a few seconds he said: "Thanks Dad. It's OK now." I stood up and saw by the look on his face that he was happy. I left the room, puzzled, and told my wife about what had just happened. "Funny," she said, "he asked me to do the same thing yesterday." This lasted for a week, and then suddenly stopped. Ten years later, Tom had problems finding his place in the family, specifically in relation to me. It was serious enough that we decided to go see a psychologist. After two sessions, she asked to see me alone. In our discussion, she recommended that I physically wrestle with my boys. So I did. After a few days – and a lot of muscle cramps for me – all the symptoms of Tom's distress had once again disappeared.

When children feel that they are not touched, embraced, or held enough, they adopt a specific behavior – e.g., charming, helpful, tearful, aggressive, provocative, whining, sulky, etc. – to force others to engage in skin contact. Children do this because they know deep inside, as we all do, that if they are not touched, they will die, first psychologically, and then physically. In order to avoid this fatal outcome, they always find a way to be touched, even if it is not the best way, unconsciously striving for any form of physical contact, from pats, kisses, and embraces, to spanks, slaps, and even blows.

Science has confirmed this terrible conclusion, establishing a clear link between the lack of physical contact and aggressive behaviors. The more people are touched with love in their childhood and teen years, the less physically and verbally aggressive they are once adults.[140] In a comparative study conducted in 1981 in American and French playgrounds, researchers observed that French children were touched six times more often than their American peers. In the same two countries, adolescents belonging to the same socioeconomic classes and to the same ethnic groups were studied in McDonald's restaurants. The adolescents were observed for a period of twenty minutes, their behavior recorded every ten seconds. While in France adolescents regularly caressed one another's backs, arms, hands, and necks, American teenagers preferred self-touch, playing with their hands and hair. Scientists concluded that this could be one of the reasons why the level of violence was lower in France.[141]

Premature babies, who are caressed for five minutes every hour for ten days, regain birth weight faster, sleep better, cry less, are more vigorous, and leave the hospital faster.[142] Adult patients, who are touched by their doctor during an office visit, keep their promise to take their prescribed medication more often than patients who have not been touched.[143] When elderly people who suffer from Parkinson's disease are touched gently while they eat, after only three weeks they show a higher ability to provide for themselves than their colleagues who were not touched.[144]

Touching is as beneficial for our physical health as for our mental one. In popular language people who have a hard time believing without seeing are often nicknamed *doubting Thomases*. This expression is based on a very limited knowledge of the Bible. The New Testament reports that after his crucifixion, Jesus of Nazareth showed himself to his disciples, and that, because the apostle Thomas was not there, he did not believe it. What people forget, however, is that the apostles not only saw and heard Jesus, but he also requested that each one of them come forth and touch his hands and feet, to feel his skin with their own skin. Anybody can question the divinity of Jesus, but nobody can challenge his complete expertise in communication. We believe that we can be tricked by what we see or hear – what we commonly call hallucinations – and we also believe that touching is a surer way to know what is real. The expression: *Pinch me, I want to see if I'm dreaming* embodies this belief, even if this trick is not entirely infallible as we can dream that we are dreaming, suspect it, pinch ourselves to wake up, wake up from the dream we are dreaming, to wake up later in reality with or without a bruise.[145] Simply put: it is impossible to resist the urge to touch things[146] to see if they are real.[147] A drive we all experience when we see a sign posted on a fence which reads in red *Wet Paint*.[148]

What does this have to do with communication?

We gather information not only through our ears and eyes, but also through our skin. Our skin constantly feed our brain with tons of data which influences our decisions, even if unconsciously. The weight, texture, and hardness of objects, for example, impact the way we see and interact with the world. When recruiters are presented with CVs on a heavy clipboard, the candidates they interview are rated as more suitable for the job than when the clipboard is light. When a group of people is requested to complete a five-piece puzzle, there is more coordination, and less competition between the participants when the puzzle has a smooth surface than when it is covered with rough sandpaper. Our behavior changes not only when we actively touch an object, but also when we are passively touched by it. For instance, participants are less willing to change their offer or to make a new decision during negotiations when they sit on hard wooden chairs than on soft cushioned seats.[149]

In a famous experiment led by Williams and Bargh, participants were welcomed by a lady who asked them in the elevator to hold her cup of coffee while she was writing down their name. Being primed for just a few seconds, sometimes holding hot coffee, sometimes iced coffee, participants arrived in a room, where they were given a questionnaire, and were asked to judge their host on ten bipolar personality traits. Despite the fact that the woman in the elevator was not aware of what the experiment was about, and even if the participants were not aware of the influence the temperature of the coffee had on their judgment, when the coffee was warm they automatically evaluated their host as having a warm personality – friendly, helpful, generous, caring, and trustworthy – and when the coffee was cold, the very same host was perceived as unpleasant, inconsiderate, and distant.[150]

Would the results of this experiment be different with Deaf people? Possibly, as Deaf people are more conscious of collecting data through their skin. During a course, as we were having lunch in a restaurant, the Deaf facilitator's knife accidentally squeaked on his plate. His Deaf colleague, who was sitting on the other side of the table, signed to him that he was making unpleasant noises with his knife, and asked him to stop. The Hearing participant I was chatting with saw it, stopped talking, and looked at me as if I was the worst con artist he had ever met:

"They aren't deaf!?" he asked in a half dubious, half angry tone.
"Of course they are," I replied defensively.
"How can they hear a knife squeaking, then?"
"I don't know," I replied honestly. "Ask them."

Using mime to communicate, the participant asked my Deaf colleagues the question. The one who had *heard* the squeaking knife carefully observed the mime, then he placed his hand flat on the table, and started to shake it, meaning: "Vibrations. I felt it."

Gabriel: Vibrations are indeed a key source of information for us.
Bruno: Can you give me an example?
Gabriel: When I was a teenager my parents had an apartment in Paris. We lived on the 7th floor. One day, I was in my bedroom with Pierre, a Hearing friend, and we were waiting for one of our friends to go to the movies. We were chatting about all sorts of things when suddenly I stopped to put my jacket on. Our friend had just entered the building.
Bruno: How did you know?
Gabriel: That's the question Pierre asked me too. I told him that I had felt the vibration of the elevator starting on the ground floor.
Bruno: Six floors below?
Gabriel: I know [smile]. Pierre also thought I was joking. He couldn't feel, or hear anything. So he started to make fun of me. When I felt the vibration of the elevator reaching the 7th floor, I went to the door and opened it. My friend was standing there, in front of the door, his index finger poised ready to ring the doorbell. Pierre was shocked. His smile turned into a nervous grin.

Henry: Hearing people often ask me how I can so easily detect the presence of someone who is not in my field of vision.
Bruno: That *is* a good question. How do you do it?

Henry: It depends. It can be the vibration of a creak I feel through my feet when I'm standing on a wood floor, a little puff of air which hits the back of my neck when someone opens a door, or when I'm reading a newspaper, the voice of someone vibrating on the membrane of an open page.[151]

Deaf people capture data through their skin. Hearing people do as well, even if they are not fully aware of it. Hearing people understand speech not only by listening to sound waves and looking at lip movement, but also by feeling and decoding tiny puffs of air bumping against their skin. Researchers have demonstrated that when people hear the sound *ba* and *da* while at the same time receiving a little puff of air on their neck, they interpret the sound they hear as *pa* and *ta*, two sounds which, to be produced, are accompanied by stronger bursts of air.[152]

Touch to connect

One day, as I was sitting in my office, I client came to see me. I could see by her way of walking that something was wrong. She sat down and we started talking. She was clearly making an effort to hold back her tears. I listened carefully to her, but despite my active listening, she still held back. I decided to take a risk. Slowly and carefully, I slightly touched her forearm with my fingertips for a few seconds. This simple physical touch was all that was missing. The dam broke; she burst into tears. She cried and cried and cried. I remained silent. Whenever she started to calm down, she would say "Oh, Bruno, you're so nice," and then she would burst into tears once more. When there was not a single tear left in her body, she took a big breath, and started to explain what her problem was, but I had a hard time focusing on what she was saying. Something obscure was bothering me. So I asked:

"Why did you say several times that I was *so* nice?"
"Because you are."
"What did I do to make you believe that I'm nice?"
"You allow me to express myself. No one else does."
"No one?"
"No. No one. Not my husband, nor my kids, not my manager, not my friends. You're the only one. They all say the same thing. I shouldn't complain. I shouldn't cry. I should always be nice, positive, and happy. You're the only one who allows me to really express myself."
"…"

I thought about this for a moment. What gave her the feeling that I was allowing her to really express herself? Certainly, the others were not preventing her from talking. So what was the difference? Then I understood. A slight touch on the arm, accompanied by considerate silence meant to her: "Tell me how you feel. I'm listening to you. I do care."

In communication, touch is that important. And, strangely enough, it is sometimes easier to touch complete strangers or pat animals than the people we really love: our partner and our children. This is an odd behavior when we know that touching not only improves our connection with others, but also the way we perform together.

Touch to perform

Touch also helps people to perform better both as individuals and as a group. Psychologists have demonstrated that when students are touched during classes they show superior results on their exams than their colleagues who have not been touched.[153] Similarly, when students are briefly touched on the forearm by a teacher during an exercise, the number of students who volunteer afterwards to go to the blackboard dramatically increases.[154] In school tasks, touching improves positive behaviors such as taking a book to read, or checking information in a dictionary by 20%, and reduces disruptive behaviors such as getting up without permission or fighting with a classmate by 60%.[155]

This is not only true in school, but also in sports, business, and love. In 2009, by analyzing 294 players of the NBA, researchers demonstrated that the most successful basketball teams are those with players who touch one another more regularly, and that the best and most talented players are those who touch and are touched the most often.[156] In the street, touching people increases the number of responses a surveyor gets.[157] In a restaurant, a waitress who briefly touches customers on the hand or the shoulder receives bigger tips than waitresses who don't, regardless of the customer's gender, the restaurant's atmosphere, or the dining experience.[158] And when potential consumers are touched at the entrance of a supermarket – for example when they are given a flyer – they stay in the store longer, spend more money, and rate the shop higher than the competition.[159] Studies also show that light and short term touch increases success in courtship. A man in a nightclub who asks a woman to dance while touching her forearm for less than two seconds has more of a chance of having the woman accept than someone who doesn't touch her.[160]

Differences between people

Bruno: In the West, one of the most common ways to initiate contact with someone is by shaking hands.

Helen: This is so important for me as I'm Deaf and blind. Just by shaking hands, I know who I'm dealing with. I've met people so empty of joy that when I shake their hands it feels like going into a blizzard.

Bruno: And can you detect happy people too?

Helen: Of course. Those people have sunbeams in their hands. When I touch them it fills my heart with joy. Their hands still have the same touch as that of children. I understand people as much by shaking hands as you do by looking in their eyes.[161]

I remember two very special handshakes I received in my life. The first was when for the first time, someone shook my hand with two hands, one clasped, and the other kindly and respectfully holding my wrist. More than twenty years later I still remember how important I felt during that handshake. The second one I remember is a handshake an Indian trainee gave me, grabbing my hand after a course, and for about fifteen minutes walking around in the hallways of my company, chatting with me without letting go of my hand. I remember the size of his hand, the moistness of it. I remember feeling so uncomfortable, sweating, but still not withdrawing my hand to avoid hurting his feelings. Just like fingerprints, there are as many handshakes as there are people. None are neutral. They all send a message. They all reveal who you really are. From Kant's perspective, your hand is the extension of your mind. Here are a few examples:

The Business Handshake: Your hand is dry, your grip is firm, and the shake is made of only two movements. You look the other straight in the eyes which sends the message: "you can trust me."

The Political Handshake: You have white teeth, a big smile, and you look at everybody except the person you are shaking hands with. It is as if you were looking for journalists.

The Four Hands Handshake: The right hands are clasped, and the left hands cover the handshake. This handshake lasts longer than the political one, to allow even more time for journalists to take a good picture.

The Buddy Handshake: Your hand meets the other person's hand profoundly. The complete surface of your palm is in contact with the other's palm. Your hand is warm and firm. There is no shaking.

The Grab and Pull Handshake: You grab the other's hand and pull the person towards you with energy. Sometimes you add a tap on the back. This handshake is perceived by the other as dominant and paternalistic.

The Grab and Push Handshake: The twin brother of the previous handshake. At the end of this handshake, you push the other's hand away from you, which may give the other person a feeling of rejection.

The Grab and Guide Handshake: Another member of the grab family. You grab the hand, you keep it firmly in yours, and guide the other towards a place you have decided upon. This is the control freak's handshake.

The Bone Cruncher Handshake: You squeeze the other person's hand as hard as you can. The goal is to show that you are the boss by seeing tears and submission in the other person's eyes.

The Fingertips Handshake: Only the first phalanges enter in contact with the other's hand, and then you withdraw your fingers as quickly as possible. It seems like you are afraid of germs.

The Teacup Handshake: Also called the Arthritis Handshake. Your hand is cupped, creating a pocket of air between the palms. Your fingers point at the ground and you avoid eye contact. Are you hiding something?

The Compassionate Handshake: As you are shaking the other person's hand, you place your left hand on the upper part of the other's arm or shoulder. If sincere, it is touching. If fake, it creates repulsion.

The Dead Fish Handshake: One of the most famous. A crazy surgeon has taken all the bones out of your hand. The shaking movement is fully initiated and controlled by the other person. Your message is "I'm dead."

The Secret Handshake: Includes high fives, fist bumps, gang and secret orders' handshakes. This handshake works only when both people know the sequence. If not, the person who doesn't know it always feels stupid.

The Wrist Handshake: Your hand is dirty, so you shake the other's hand with your wrist.

The Left Handshake: Your right hand is busy, so you use your left hand. There is only one case in which you can allow yourself to shake hands with your left: when you don't have a right one.[162]

Some handshakes are pleasant, others are not. All of them reveal who you are, your mood, and what your intention is at that specific moment. Do you present your hand with your palm open, facing up (I am not a threat to you, look, I have no weapon), or facing down (showing your power and domination like the Nazi salute)? Is your grip light, firm, or crushing? Whatever way you shake hands, know that people will remember it. Worse, you might be reduced in their mind to the handshake you gave them. Some people say that there is no correlation between a handshake and someone's personality. Maybe they are right, but whatever the truth about this assumption, no one can deny the fact that every handshake leaves the other person with a certain impression. A colleague of mine shakes hands mixing several of the handshakes described above. His right hand moves fast towards you. He then pinches your hand with only the tip of his fingers, his hand forming a cup, his fingers pointing down, and then, he pushes your hand away from him, as if suddenly remembering that you are a leper. Every time we shake hands, I must make an effort to convince myself that it is my hand he is rejecting, not me. Your handshake is never neutral. And it is the only real business card you have. What is yours like?

Differences between cultures

Of course, skin contact varies according to culture, gender, social status, and relationship. If you were to observe people sitting at the terrace of a café and record how often they touch each other, you would count on average 180 body contacts an hour in San Juan, Puerto Rico, 110 in Paris, France, 2 in Gainesville, Florida, USA, and 0 in London, England.[163] In India you would see men walking hand in hand in the street; in France you would see them kissing on the cheeks, sometimes up to five times; and in the UAE you would see them greeting one another by rubbing their noses like Eskimos who are in love. In 1989, every Westerner watched with incredulity when Erich Honecker kissed Soviet President Mikhail Gorbachev on the lips when he landed in East Berlin to attend the celebrations of the 40th anniversary of the East German state. In 2009, at Buckingham Palace, every British person saw with horror when US First Lady Michelle Obama put her hand on Queen Elizabeth II's back, as she would have done with her grandmother.

Different cultures, different touching rules, one of the most visible being between the Deaf and Hearing worlds. Contrary to Hearing people, Deaf people often communicate by touching, to get someone's attention, to build a three dimensional image together – like two sculptors working on the same block of clay – or to put an end to a conversation by kindly or playfully holding the other person's hands to enforce visual silence.

Deaf people also hug and kiss all the time. While Hearing people tend to reserve their hugs for close family members, or only for specific events – after a long break or for emotional situations such as births, marriages, and funerals – Deaf people hug when they meet, when they part, morning, afternoon, evening, as often in their private lives as in their professional ones: they hug family, friends, colleagues, and even suppliers and clients. Not only do they hug more than Hearing people, but they also hug differently. As Deaf people feel more comfortable with their body, the amount of body contact between two Deaf people hugging is greater than between that of two Hearing people. This is so true that Deaf people often compare Hearing hugs to an upside-down V shape.[164]

Clarisse: An advantage we have over Hearing people is that we quickly see when something is wrong with others. When you ask how someone is doing and the answer is "Fine," we know right away if it's not true.

Bruno: With some effort Hearing people can do this to. But when there is a discrepancy between what is said and what is felt, we still have to initiate a conversation, which is not at all easy. Sometimes it can take several days before one finds the courage to talk to someone else.

Clarisse: On this point, once again, Deaf people have an advantage. Sign Language helps us to deal with a problem faster than Hearing people.

Bruno: Really? How?

Clarisse: When I've been hurt, I stand behind my husband and pass my arms under his arms in order to have my hands in front of him. Then, I tell him about how I feel. In this position, I don't have to look in his eyes – which would be hard because of the emotions – and when I sign *hurt*, he doesn't know yet if I'm talking about him, about me, or about us.[165]

Bruno: No opposition, no accusation, no aggression, while maintaining physical contact at the same time. That must help you to reconnect.

Clarisse: Possibly. This position helps us to physically become one. I'm him, and he is me. If he has been mean to me, I will simply sign *mean*, and he will not feel aggressed as I am pointing as much towards him as towards myself. In other words, we both bear responsibility for the situation. Similarly, when I sign *sad*, I say that I also recognize that he's sad about the situation. Expressed in this way, no one feels accused. Both have hurt and been hurt. Both need to be reassured and loved by the other person. When we communicate that way, it is no longer me against him or him against me, but us against our difficulty expressing our emotions.

Bruno: And how long does this ritual last?

Clarisse: Not long. It's only a bridge to help us move on to a face-to-face conversation, a useful bridge to move from conflict to resolution.

I was so amazed by such an unusual and mature way of dealing with conflict that I was curious to know more about their intimacy. The most difficult, profound, or tender discussions I have ever had with my wife, have always been late at night, in bed, and in the dark. How could Deaf people do this? I asked Marylène if she was comfortable having this discussion. She was.

Bruno: How do you communicate when you are in bed, in the dark?

Clarisse: First by vibration. The vibrations of the mattress are not the same when the other person is coughing, laughing, or crying. We also touch the other person's face to read emotions. It's easy, pleasant, and very precise when you are used to it. Or we talk into the other's hand. I take his hand and sign in it. Sometimes I also do it on his back. Of course, these conversations aren't very in depth, nor do they last for hours.

Bruno: Why do you have them then?

Clarisse: To finish a conversation. To express emotions we were not able to express in the light. In daylight, we don't communicate as much by touching. But when the lights are off, we are forced to touch each other if we want to keep on interacting. It's very pleasant. It's a nice, soft, and progressive way to leave each other… until we meet again the next day.

Research shows that when couples are engaged in more touching, they report more satisfaction with their relationship. As Deaf people touch, stroke, rub, caress, cuddle, pat, tap, hug, and embrace day and night, does it mean that Deaf couples are stronger? Science still needs to confirm or infirm this hypothesis. But whatever the result, there is a great lesson to be learned from the Deaf world: reconnection does not happen through words, but through touching. This is where the difficulty lies: in being able to touch, and to accept being touched back, even if it is only through a light touch of the finger tips. Only then, can real communication start again.

This might be one of the greatest Deaf assets. And this is certainly one of the most important lessons I have learned from them. Because of the nature of my job, I regularly travel around the world for long periods of time. And despite the love Magali and I share, it always takes us – specifically me – some time, from a few hours to a day or two, to really reconnect when I come home. Like any Hearing couple, we would use oral communication to reconnect. "How did the kids behave?" "How was Dubai?" "Did you have a nice flight?" Completely artificial, empty, and emotionless communication, which in fact had the effect of widening the gap that had been created by time and distance even more. Today, things are different. When I come back home after a long trip, we manage our schedules to make sure that we are alone for an hour or two and, without talking, we touch. Once done, we are reconnected, and our relationship is as strong as before my departure. Touch as often as you can, as long as there is love, respect, and trust.

Are there any exceptions?

In a Leadership course I was delivering to trainees who came from all over Europe, a Brit explained to the group that because of his culture he would never let his manager touch him. I rephrased:

"If *today*, your manager came to you and put his hand on your shoulder while talking to you, how would you react?"
"I would quickly stand up and move a meter or two away from him."
"Would you tell him that you didn't like it?"
"I might."
"Would you file a complaint?"
"If he did it again, probably."
"OK. Now let's imagine that you've been working for several years for another manager. That manager is the best manager you've ever had. He has a vision and shares it in an exciting way. He likes your work and expresses this regularly. He's honest, clear, and straightforward in his dealings. He respects people, and in return he's respected by all. He's a role model to you. Imagine that one day, as you are going through a difficult time, he put his hand on your shoulder and gives you words of encouragement. How would you react?"
"…" [silence].

It is never upbringing or culture which prevents us from touching one another. It is a lack of mutual respect and trust.

1. Every human being needs to touch and to be touched. It is a vital need.
2. The way we touch and are touched influences the way we perceive and consequently interpret our environment.
3. When we are touched respectfully, we feel more positive about ourselves and about the world.
4. When people genuinely touch with a positive intention in mind, it always increases their desire to interact.

Deaf Tip n°11: Get in touch
Exercises

- Teaching others is the best way to learn. Share something you have learned in this chapter with at least three friends, colleagues, or members of your family.
- What do you touch regularly? Why?
- Who do you touch regularly? Make a list. How would you rate your level of trust and respect?
- Would you like to add other people to this list? What would you need to do in order to be able to touch these people?
- When you touch people this week, make an effort to be more conscious when you do it.
- Observe people in the street or at the terrace of a café. Do they touch? How often? For how long? How? What would you like to do similarly or differently when you are with your loved ones?
- Take more time and find more opportunities to touch your loved ones.
- Play the following game regularly with your children: write words with your finger in their hand or on their back, and ask them to decipher what you wrote.
- What type of handshake do you have? Ask three people to describe it to you. Are you happy with it? If not, change it.
- When you shake hands with people this week, change your handshake, and observe people's reactions.
- Buy a book on massage or take a class with your partner. Buy a good quality massage oil with an exotic fragrance like coconut or vanilla, and practice massage at least once a month.
- When you have an argument with someone you love, don't try to reconcile by talking. Try to reconnect by touching gently.
- What could you do to improve your communication with the three people you selected in the introduction?
- Practice, practice, practice.
- Once done, move on to another chapter.

Personal Notes

Speak your mind, even if your voice shakes.
Maggie Kuhn, American Activist

Deaf Tip n°12
Say what you think

I was in an elevator, ready to press the 3rd floor button, when I heard someone walking down the hall. I held the door of the elevator and waited. A lady weighing about 300 pounds appeared. I was in trouble. Not because she was overweight, but because I was with Tom, who was only five at the time. I knew exactly what would happen. I asked the lady which floor she was going to, hoping she would answer the 1st floor, but she was on the 4th, one floor above us. I pressed the button and waited for trouble. As soon as the doors closed, Tom pointed in the direction of the lady – in a twenty square foot elevator pointing means touching her belly with his finger– and said loudly "Dad, why is she so fat?" I remained silent, of course, pretending that I hadn't heard. It took about 20 minutes for the elevator to reach the 3nd floor – or at least it felt like it. I politely said goodbye, and as soon as the door of our apartment was closed, I did some *socialization* with the boy just to make sure it would never happen again.

Years later, having matured a little bit, looking back on this anecdote, I wonder, what was wrong with my son's question? After all, the lady was bigger than most of the people he had seen before and he wanted to understand. Is there something wrong with trying to understand the world? Is there something wrong with being big? If not, why then is it forbidden to talk about it openly? Why do we have to be so careful?

In the Hearing world straight and explicit speech or questions are frowned upon, often being seen as offensive. Hearing teenagers follow a long and complex process before asking their parents if they can sleep at a friend's house. Hearing employees prepare their managers for weeks before asking for a pay rise. And when someone asks Hearing people for their point of view, instead of saying what they really think, they often try to guess what the other person wants to hear. If she asks: "Do you like my new dress?" He answers: "I love it." If he says: "I'm getting old." She replies: "You haven't changed a bit." And when a boss wants to know: "How was my speech?" The assistant quickly reply: "It was so clear, so powerful!"

We wrap our thoughts in acceptable wording from morning to night to preserve our relationships with others. And it is only when someone starts a sentence with: "To tell you the truth…" "To be completely transparent…" "To be frank…" or "To be honest with you…" that we suddenly realize that everything that was said previously was pure embellishment or simply lies. Contrary to this Hearing behavior, Deaf people consider anything which interferes with speed, clarity, and precision as inappropriate.

Daniella: Yesterday I had breakfast downtown and couldn't brush my teeth. Then, I ran from one meeting to the next until 4 PM. I literally spoke to dozens of people.
Bruno: And?
Daniella: And I came across one of my Deaf friends. The first thing she told me was that I had something stuck in my teeth! I had had food stuck in my teeth since 8 o'clock and everybody saw it but no one dared to tell me!
Bruno: No one?
Daniella: No Hearing person I mean. It seems you need to be Deaf to feel the right to talk straight.

In the Deaf world, to say things as they are does not amount to being rude. "I don't like your new dress," "you hair is turning grey," or "I didn't understand a thing about what you said" is not considered as impolite if it is what you think, what you have observed, or what you have heard. Deaf communication is based on two simple principles: describing what you see and saying what you think.

Describe what you see

Valentin: Deaf people always describe what they see and accept what is being described. Let's imagine that I meet a friend I haven't seen for years, and that I barely recognize him because he lost his hair. If I was a Hearing person the conversation would go like this:

"Long time no see! How are you?"

"Fine. I'm so happy to see you again."

"Me too. You're looking great!"

"Thanks."

"But something is different."

"What?"

"I don't know. Did you change your glasses?"

"No. They're the same."

"Oh. Did you grow a beard, then?"

"No, no. I always had that beard. Oh… You mean that I've lost my hair?!"

"Oh, no. No. Not at all."

This conversation could go on forever, with hundreds of understatements, Hearing people never say what they really think, or what everyone can see is obvious.

Bruno: And this situation would be different between two Deaf friends?

Valentin: Of course. Completely different. The very same situation with two Deaf people would go like this:

"Long time no see! How are you?"

"Fine. I'm so happy to see you again."

"Geez. You lost all your hair!"

"I know."

Bruno: And they would not become enemies, after that?

Valentin: [smile] No, why? It isn't being aggressive. We just describe what we see. It's faster. Nothing is hidden. Not even feelings.

Bruno: Why do you think Hearing and Deaf people are so different?

Valentin: I think that Hearing people believe that they must comply with the norm. If they have irregular teeth, a crooked nose, or Dumbo ears, they just can't live with it. They have to go for surgery. And if they can't, they make sure that no one makes any reference to it. For Deaf people it is a lot easier

Bruno: Why?

Valentin: Because we have never been in the norm.

Bruno: What do you mean?

Valentin: The media dictates to society what is beautiful and what is ugly. And they have always placed us in the ugly box with all the people who are different, with the people who are disturbing. So why should we comply with rules which have been decreed by people who reject us?

Bruno: A life away from the mediacracy sounds like freedom to me. And it looks so much easier. One of my friends waited several months before daring to ask a colleague if she was pregnant. He was so afraid of making a blunder.

Valentin: In my world, it would be much simpler. I would say: "Are you pregnant or did you put on some weight?" And, if she was Deaf, she would simply answer the question.

Bruno: But if she was Hearing, and had put on some weight, she would hate you for the rest of your life [laugh]!

Listening to my Deaf colleague, I felt Hearing people were like porcelain dolls. So sensitive, so fragile. Fighting against their greatest fear: rejection, and finding a way to avoid it: normalization. If we all had the same shape, the same haircut, the same regular white teeth, and the same cell phone, how could we be rejected? It would be a perfect world. Except for one small detail: who would want to live in such a uniform world? And would it be possible to be happy in such a world? Happiness only exists because of sadness, beauty because of ugliness. If everyone was beautiful, then no one would be. And if we were never sad, then we would not even know what happiness is. Besides, how could we distinguish anything in such a standardized environment? At least, when Deaf people talk about someone who is 5 feet tall, weighs 180 pounds, is bald, with a double chin, a wart on the nose, and a broken tooth everyone knows who they are referring to. In fact, Deaf descriptions are so precise, and so true, that they often make you laugh… except, of course, when they are describing you!

Some years ago, I recruited a trainer for my team. Be it in coaching, training, or facilitation, he exceeded all of our clients' expectations. He was perfect… except for his eyebrows. His eyebrows were very long on top, and pointed up like Mr. Spock's. Day after day I wondered if he knew. I wondered if he purposely styled them that way. I wondered why he didn't cut them. I even wondered if he was a Vulcan. But, of course, being Hearing by culture, I never dared to ask him any of these questions. Then, we took Sign Language classes together. And, as is the custom, after a few weeks we received our sign names: a swift gesture which represents you more precisely than your own name. Millions of Hearing people have the same name, with no correlation with who they are. So we sat in a circle, and each of us received his or her sign name, always accompanied by a lot of laughter. When it was my colleague's turn, our Deaf teacher pinched his eyebrows between his thumb and index finger and pulled them up quickly. Everyone burst out laughing, including my colleague. I was relieved. I now felt that I could ask him all the questions I had had for the last few weeks. What a surprise to find out that all my fears of shocking, hurting, or upsetting him were only in my head. He was conscious of his weird eyebrows and completely at ease talking about them.

For Deaf people sign names are never negative or mean. They are simply the most economical and precise way to define someone. Hearing people might find them brutal, but this perception of brutality reveals more about Hearing culture than Deaf culture. As expressed by David Wright, Deaf dealings "may appear outrageously direct; their handshakes are ungloved. They have a naïveté, and also a plain honesty of intent, that often makes the polite wrappings-up of ordinary people seem, by contrast, hypocritical."[166]

Bruno: How do you choose your sign name?
Mathylde: You don't. Other people like your parents or your friends do it for you. If it was not the case, all the guys would call themselves: Handsome, Stylish, or Muscular-Build, and the girls: Beautiful-Eyes, Sexy-Voice, or Full-Lips.
Bruno: So, how do people choose your sign name?
Mathylde: It's often linked to your body, your behavior, or your name. Sometimes it's a mix of all three. But it's always something which stands out. I've a friend who's called Hook-Nose, one called Big-Belly, and another one called Thumb-Under-the-Nose because of the dewdrops he wipes from his nose several times a day.

Bruno: And you, David, what's your sign name?
David: [smile] It's made with a fist clenched at the back of the head, fingers exploding upwards to represent my un-brushed hair sticking out.[167]

Bruno: I hope Deaf people only do this amongst themselves.
Lucie: Oh no, we also do it with Hearing people. I know a smart guy who has invented a lot of things but who is so awkward with his hands that we call him Two-Hands-Hanging-Dead-in-Front-of-the-Chest. His girlfriend has bulging eyes. Her sign is done by placing the two hands in front of the eyes in the shape of a bowl. But of course, they don't know about it. We are cautious with Hearing people. We don't want to hurt their feelings. Hearing people don't like to hear about the unusual aspects of their body or behavior, even if everybody, including themselves, is aware of it.

Bruno: And if you don't like your sign name, can you change it?
Charlie: It's possible, but very difficult. And the new name is not always better than the previous one.
Bruno: That sounds rough.

Charlie: Not really. Your sign name gives you a unique identity, and as it's given by people who know you, it creates a bond between you and them. In fact, you should be cautious with people who don't have a sign name. If they don't have one, it's either because they don't have any friends, or because they're so dull that they simply don't deserve one.[168]

Say what you think

This straightforward form of communication goes against the Hearing political correctness launched in the 70s, supported by the media and relayed by the masses, encouraging people to avoid using any language which refers to only one ethnic group, to avoid overly-cautious racial descriptions, to avoid the use of gender, to avoid any reference to a person's age, to avoid any offensive expression about their physical or mental abilities, to avoid the use of specific religious wording when people from another religion or without religion are present, to avoid any allusion to social classes, and to avoid any reference to sexual orientation. When I read this literature or hear similar recommendations, I suddenly feel very tired and think that silence might be the best way to avoid making a mistake. Political correctness doesn't fight intolerance for the simple reason that it is intolerant in the first place to forbid freedom of speech. And, contrary to what might have been the objective at the beginning, political correctness does not help at all.[169] If you are not cautious enough you are guilty, and if you are overly cautious, you are guilty as well. Don't say *God bless you* when someone sneezes, in case that person is an atheist. Try *Gesundheit*. Of course, the word is not English, but at least it does not refer to God and you will not offend your friend, except, of course, if your friend fought the Germans during WWII.

Seriously, do we really believe that racism, sexism, and other forms of hate and rejection will disappear by replacing old words with new ones? Does changing the word *fat* into *corpulent* resolve the problem of obesity in our overfed Western society? Replacing an unpleasant word with a pleasant one, doesn't make an unpleasant situation become pleasant. At best, it gives some psychological comfort to people. Senior citizens might indeed feel younger than elderly people, welfare recipients better off than free-loaders, children at risk less threatening than teenage thugs. Executives might prefer to resign than to be fired, employees to have a growing experience than to be sacked, consumers might prefer to buy a pre-owned car than a used one, we might all prefer to pass away than to die, but the result is always pretty much the same. Replacing an unpleasant word with a pleasant one doesn't make an unpleasant situation become pleasant.

How efficient is it to move carefully and slowly while in a conversation, maneuvering between susceptibilities, looking at others to see how they react to adapt what we say accordingly? What is the quality of a relationship and of communication when a dialogue is not natural? Deaf people don't ask themselves all these questions. They don't put so much pressure on themselves. They don't hide behind soft language. They don't struggle to find the most diplomatic words, hoping that others will guess what they really mean. They just say what they think, and describe what they see.

Since the beginning of this book, I have used the word Deaf, and I do so in training courses and conferences. I am always amused when afterwards Hearing people come to see me, recommending that I be more cautious with the words I use. "You shouldn't say Deaf," they tell me, it would be better to use *hard-of-hearing, hearing challenged* or *hearing impaired*. When this happens, I always ask them two questions. First: "Do you know any Deaf people?" To this question, most of them answer in the negative. Second: "What do you think Deaf people would like to be called?" to which they always reply that they don't know.[170] Then, I refrain from giving them the answer and encourage them to go and ask a Deaf person. People who are born deaf, find words such as *hearing impaired* insulting. "Why don't you call me deaf? Look! I'm not hard of hearing! I'm deaf!" Deaf people are not impaired, or challenged, and they haven't lost anything. To lose something you had to have had it in the first place. And in any case, is there something wrong with being hearing, deaf, tall, small, fat, skinny, black, or white? If not, why then are we so cautious about using these words? Words and signs are never good or bad, right or wrong. Only the intention of the people using them is. "You're crazy" can be an insult, or a beautiful declaration of love. A man might use politically correct words, and have the worst sexist thoughts. Another might use gender-based titles, but have the deepest respect for women.

Obviously, we should all make an effort to avoid hurting, excluding, or demeaning others through the way we talk. But no more than others should make an effort to avoid feeling hurt, excluded, or demeaned for the slightest reason. And if some people don't like this rule, why should you care? Real friends and interesting people will always appreciate your honesty, even if sometimes it is hard to hear. They will feel comfortable with you because they will know where you stand. They will trust you because they will know that what you say is what you think. They will respect you because they will know that your intention is never to hurt or to flatter, but to express your honest point of view. I don't know how many friends I have, but I know that I have at least one. I know it because one day he took me aside, looked me straight in the eyes and said "Bruno, you have become an asshole." It requires a lot of love, courage, and political incorrectness to talk that way. And I believe that this love, courage, and political incorrectness expressed to me on that day saved my soul, and my relationships with my wife and my children, because it woke me up, and forced me to change.

Make an oath

For some people, the hardest word to pronounce is *no* because of their fear of rejection. This fear is surprising as we have all been through a phase in our lives – the terrible twos – during which we said *no* to everything and everyone and still received a lot of love in return. So what happened? When did we move from the impossibility of saying *yes* to the impossibility of saying *no*? Why have we invented over the years all sorts of words and strategies to say *no* without really having to say it: *Yes but..., yes and no..., it depends..., well..., maybe..., not sure..., why not..., I'll give it some thought..., we'll see..., let's talk about it tomorrow...,* etc.? It is Thursday evening. You have just turned your computer off. You have been working on a difficult project for the last six months during which time your family has not seen much of you. You have promised your spouse and children that tonight you will take them out to a nice restaurant and then to the movies. It is six o'clock. If you leave now, you can still make it. As you put your jacket on, your boss, who you respect a lot, opens your office door. You can see panic on his face. He tells you: "I know that you're about to leave. But I have to deliver a presentation tomorrow at 8 AM to the Board of Executives and I'm missing some information. You're the only one who has it on your computer. Can you stay a bit longer?" You know that a bit longer in your boss's language means at least another hour. What do you reply?... Most of us would smile and say: "Yes, of course" or even worse: "Of course. No problem!" while everything inside of us is screaming "Noooo!!!"

For some people the hardest word to pronounce is *no*, but for others, it is *yes*. A manager I was coaching was always complaining about her salary. During one of our coaching sessions, I could see that something was wrong. She finally explained that she had just had an interview with her manager who had asked her if she wanted a pay raise. "What did you say?" I asked anxiously. "I said no," and she started to cry. Who would say *no* to a pay raise? Well, more people than we think. People, for example, who were raised in a family where talking about money was forbidden. Or people who need the job or the recognition from their manager so much that their constant message is "Look, I'm a good worker, and in addition I'm cheap!"

Actually, the problem is not so much the inability to say *yes* or *no*, but to say what we think. Your son who just got his driving license asks you to borrow your brand new car. Your sister asks you to lend her money that she will definitely pay back next month. A colleague comes to your office to collect money for the farewell gift for someone you don't really know. Your spouse wants to go out on a day where you feel so tired. What do you answer? If you say *yes* you will hate yourself. If you say *no*, they will hate you. How can you deal with these lose-lose situations better? Here are a few recommendations:

Step one: Make a personal oath. Often, we say *yes* because we haven't taken a clear, firm, and conscious commitment to what we want, or don't want in our life. And whenever you don't decide something, be sure that someone else will do it for you. To be the captain of your soul, you have to decide on how you will react in a specific situation before it occurs. Teenagers who have not taken the firm decision that they will never smoke, will inevitably accept the first cigarette when it is offered to them. What do you and don't you want to eat and drink, and how much? What do you and don't you want to watch on TV or see on the internet? How do you wish to treat and be treated by people? How much time do you want to spend at work? Do you know what the maximum number of nights you are ready to spend away from home is? No? Then be sure that you will quickly find yourself living in hotels. Do you have a precise body weight in mind that you don't want to exceed? No? Then be sure that you will put on weight that you don't want. Did you decide when you started your relationship with your spouse on the words you would never say? No? Then sooner or later you will say them, and will regret it, and not have the possibility to go back in time and erase them. If you don't set yourself clear do's and don'ts, you will automatically find yourself in situations you never thought you would be in, saying and doing things you never thought you would say or do, and not even understand how you got there.

Step two: Before saying *yes* or *no*, ask questions to be sure that you at least have a clear understanding of what you are agreeing or disagreeing to.[171] Often, when we understand someone else's request better, our feeble *yes* becomes a firm *no*, or when the ins and outs of an invitation are clarified, our obstructive *no* becomes a compassionate *yes*. Often, when we ask our requesters a few questions, they come up with their own solution, and we don't even have to say *yes* or *no* anymore.

Step three: Find your magic answer. Sometimes, even when we have made personal oaths, we still fall short because we don't know how to express our commitment to others. To avoid this situation we need to find a sentence, a magic answer, which can be used in just about any situation, and repeat it in our head until it becomes automatic. One of my sons found his magic answer at the age of four, at one of our friends' houses. We were having dinner and our host wanted to serve him spinach. The kid looked the adult straight in the eyes and with a big smile simply said "It's great, but no thank you." We were so astonished to see a little boy utter such an adult phrase, in such a kind but firm way, that we all laughed and forgot to insist. What is your magic answer? It should never be an excuse. Don't say *I can't*, say *I don't want to*. Don't say *I would love to but…* if you don't believe it. Don't say *I'm sorry* after having said *no* – specifically if you are not. Lying is never a solution. Being honest with yourself and others is.

Step four: Remember that when you say *no*, you are rejecting a request, not a person. When someone asks you to say or to do something which goes against your oaths, be firm and courageous. Don't reply by e-mail or SM. Do it face-to-face by simply using your magic answer and then stop. Don't add anything. Keep it brief.[172] Just smile kindly and wait. And if the requester doesn't get it and repeats his or her request, then use the broken record trick: repeat as needed… repeat as needed… repeat as needed… repeat as needed… And keep in mind that if people have the right to ask something, you have the right to refuse it. You have the right to say *no*, but there is no need to do it in an aggressive way. Remain kind and polite. Simply say: *no, thank you*. And if people still don't get it, then find new acquaintances who are less focused on themselves.

Deaf Tip n°12: Say what you think
Exercises

- Teaching others is the best way to learn. Share something you have learned in this chapter with at least three friends, colleagues, or members of your family.
- What do you think is the sign name that Deaf people would give you? What is the sign name they would give to the three people you selected at the beginning of this book?
- What is the most positive word you would use to describe the body, skill, or behavior of each of your children (or of the people you love)? Call them by this word, and observe their reactions.
- Observe yourself for a week: do you use expressions such as "to tell the truth"? Is so, which ones, how often, and why?
- Make a list of all the do's and don'ts which are non-negotiable for you in your personal, physical, psychological, emotional, social, spiritual, and professional lives.
- Define clear limits, with precise indicators, for each of these do's and don'ts (e.g., no more than one chocolate bar a week, minimum one compliment to one person a day, never over 70 kilos, etc.).
- Find a magic sentence which fits your personality and style. Repeat it often in your mind until you feel comfortable with it, then select an easy conflict situation to test it in. Observe the reactions of people and refine your magic answer if necessary.
- In your next encounters or interactions with people, listen carefully to your thoughts and to what you say. Measure the gap between the two and then, step by step, reduce the gap by saying things which are closer to your thoughts.
- What could you do to improve your communication with the three people you selected in the introduction?
- Practice, practice, practice.
- Once done, move on to another chapter.

Personal Notes

You cannot cause a shadow to disappear by trying to fight it,
stamp on it, or rail against it.
To cause a shadow to disappear you must shine light on it.
Shakti Gawain, American Writer

Conclusion

If insanity is, as described by Einstein, doing the same thing over and over again yet expecting different results, then we are all insane. We always hope that our environment will change without our doing anything. And whenever we are forced to really behave differently and think that we have changed, in reality we have not. We have not for the simple reason that genuine change is sustainable, and sustainability is reached only when it is a personal decision which triggers the transformation, not an external factor. When people act by mimicry, behaving like everybody else does, they have not changed. The proof is that if others were to revert to the initial behavior, they would to.

When I am at an airport gate, I am always amused to see how, when two or three people suddenly standup and move to the counter, even if there has been no announcement, nearly all the rest of the passengers start lining up. And when, after twenty minutes, feeling bored because nothing has happened, a few of them leave the line to sit down again, half of the travelers do the same thing. So it is with most of our so-called changes. Over the last decade, many people have gone green: recycling, carpooling, buying organic food, and selecting products with less packaging. Why such a dramatic change in their behavior? Have they really decided to save the planet? Or are they just following a trendy way of life stimulated by mass media propaganda? Change is an individual journey. A journey during which we often have to swim against the tide. It is a personal quest which is stimulated by one of the four following emotions, each revealing our level of psychological maturity, each informing us about how sustainable our change will be. When we change it is either because of:

Level 1: The fear of pain or punishment ("I must… otherwise…")
Level 2: A feeling of duty or responsibility ("I have to… I have no choice")
Level 3: The hope or desire for a reward ("I want to… because if I do…")
Level 4: True love, expecting nothing in return ("I love to…")

The most primitive stimulus for change is fear. Fear of pain, suffering, death, punishment, authority, failure, disappointment, rejection, or loneliness. To avoid these frightening situations, we are ready to accept change – any type of change – as long as we can escape the uncomfortable situation we are in. The problem with this stimulus, however, is that we perceive it as completely extrinsic. We believe, in other words, that we are not responsible for the situation at all and therefore do not have any control over it. Consequently, as soon as the threat decreases – fewer discussions about divorce, financial improvement of the company, a positive health diagnosis – we quickly return to our initial behavior: once again being discourteous with our spouse, lazy at work, or careless with our body.

We enter the second level of maturity when we start taking responsibility for the changes we are going through (intrinsic), even if we believe that we mainly have to do it for other people (extrinsic). This is typically the case of many new spouses, parents, or managers: "Now that I am … I have to …" The danger with this type of change, however, is that, day after day, a contained frustration grows inside of us until we can't bear it anymore and explode, discharging all of our negative emotions in the face of the people we see as responsible for our frustration.

Next comes hope, or desire, the third level of maturity. When we reach this level of psychological autonomy, we leave reactivity to behave in a proactive way. We don't run away from these situations anymore. We run towards them, hoping for some sort of reward. As this type of change is typically transactional, the stimulus is now half intrinsic, half extrinsic. We are ready to give away something because we believe that we will receive its equivalent in return (health, money, recognition, etc.). This type of change requires more maturity than the first two levels; however, the drawback remains the same: as soon as the reward is obtained, the effort disappears, and once again, we are back to square one.

In fact, real change cannot be triggered by fear, duty, or hope. It can only be brought about by love. When love is the trigger, we clearly understand the inputs and outputs of the situation. We are conscious of what people will think, say, and do in reaction to the changes we will initiate. We acknowledge that it will not be easy, but accept this. We don't change because other people are making this same change. We don't do it because other people aren't doing it. We don't change to avoid something. And we don't change to obtain something. We change simply because deep inside we know that it is the right thing to do. We don't change because we must, because we have to or because we want to, but because we love ourselves, others, and our environment enough to do it.

Here are a few examples of these four levels of maturity:

Why do you want to stop smoking?
(1) because you cough a lot and your latest lung x-rays don't look good
(2) because you are pregnant and feel responsible for the health of your baby
(3) because with the money you will save you will be able to go on vacation
(4) because you respect and love your body and that of other people so much that you don't want to poison them

Why do you follow spiritual or religious principles?
(1) because you don't want to burn in hell
(2) because you were brought up in that religion. Or maybe because you believe that these principles hold our society together
(3) because you want to receive blessings on this Earth and go to Heaven
(4) because your relationship with the Divine fills you with love

Why do you want to improve your communication?
(1) because otherwise your boss will fire you and your spouse kick you out
(2) because that is what people expect from a good manager or colleague
(3) because if you get really good at it, you will get a promotion
(4) because you enjoy feeling connected to people so much

We can improve our communication with others for many different reasons. But it is obvious that when we improve it because of love, our transformation, being more profound, becomes at the same time more sustainable. For the only true way to communicate with others is not with our voice, our ears, our eyes, or our body, but with our heart.

360° Feedback Questionnaire

Now you have read *Deaf Tips* and applied 12 new behaviors to improve your communication. But did it really improve? To find out, launch a new 360° feedback questionnaire and compare it to the first one.

Instructions

1. Make ten photocopies of the following questionnaire. Place each questionnaire in an envelope.

2. Once the photocopies are done, rate yourself on the 20 questions. To answer them, think about real situations you have been in since reading *Deaf Tips*, and be as honest as possible.

3. Give an envelope to each of the 10 people you selected at the beginning of *Deaf Tips*. Explain that you would like to see if you have improved your communication skills.

4. When you receive the results, express your gratitude to the people who answered the questionnaire.

5. Write down the results – yours and the ones received from the 10 people – on the chart following the questionnaire. Observe the discrepancies between the way you see yourself and the way others see you. Compare these results with the original results you received at the beginning of this book. Have you improved? In which areas? Where do you still need to make an effort?

360° Feedback Questionnaire

Thank you for helping me to improve my communication skills. Please read the following 24 questions carefully, thinking about concrete situations which we have been in together recently. There are no right or wrong answers. Sometimes you will be tempted to answer the way you wish I had behaved. This is not what is requested here. I would like you to describe how I actually behaved. I want to know what you observe on a regular basis. I need this information to improve. Thank you for your help, and for your honesty.

Scale:
1: I don't know
2: Rarely
3: Sometimes
4: Frequently
5: Always

01	Do I make myself available, and make you feel welcome when we talk?	①②③④⑤
02	Do I take into account the context and the situation, when I try to understand what you say?	①②③④⑤
03	Do I avoid distractions – like looking at my phone or at people walking by – when you talk to me?	①②③④⑤
04	Do I notice facial expressions (e.g., frowning), and react to them ("Let me rephrase, I don't think I was clear")?	①②③④⑤
05	Do I avoid technical wording and acronyms with people who don't know them?	①②③④⑤
06	Do I try to see through other people's eyes to feel what they feel, and understand their point of view?	①②③④⑤
07	Do I avoid guessing what you want to say by interrupting you and finishing your sentences?	①②③④⑤
08	Do I give you enough time to express what you want to say without showing signs of impatience?	①②③④⑤
09	Do I use short, simple sentences to avoid getting lost in details and endless explanations?	①②③④⑤
10	Do I adapt my language according to the people I am talking to and the situations I am in?	①②③④⑤
11	Do I know uplifting poems, quotes, or songs by heart, and do I use them regularly?	①②③④⑤

12	Do I prefer positive formulations (yes, can, do), to negative ones (no, can't, don't)?	①②③④⑤
13	Do I admit when I don't know or understand something, and do I easily ask people for help?	①②③④⑤
14	Am I more knowledgeable today than a few months ago? Do I try to learn something new every day?	①②③④⑤
15	Do I concentrate more on what you mean than on what you say?	①②③④⑤
16	Do I pay more attention to you and your needs when we talk than to me and what I want?	①②③④⑤
17	Do I often tell stories, relate anecdotes, and use visual and creative language?	①②③④⑤
18	Do I use visual supports such as my body, objects, or drawings to illustrate what I say?	①②③④⑤
19	Do I remember precisely sentences or stories you told me years ago?	①②③④⑤
20	Do I ever describe important things which happened to you long time ago?	①②③④⑤
21	Am I comfortable touching people (handshakes, hugs etc.) when appropriate?	①②③④⑤
22	Do I accept being touched by people (handshakes, hugs, etc.) when appropriate?	①②③④⑤
23	Do I say what I think even when the environment is hostile?	①②③④⑤
24	Do I say *yes* when I think yes, and *no* when I think no, instead of using circumlocutions?	①②③④⑤

Results

	1	2	3	4	5	6	7	8	9	10	Aver.	Me
Q1												
Q2												
Average for Deaf Tip n°1												
Q3												
Q4												
Average for Deaf Tip n°2												
Q5												
Q6												
Average for Deaf Tip n°3												
Q7												
Q8												
Average for Deaf Tip n°4												
Q9												
Q10												
Average for Deaf Tip n°5												
Q11												
Q12												
Average for Deaf Tip n°6												
Q13												
Q14												
Average for Deaf Tip n°7												
Q15												
Q16												
Average for Deaf Tip n°8												
Q17												
Q18												
Average for Deaf Tip n°9												
Q19												
Q20												
Average for Deaf Tip n°10												
Q21												
Q22												
Average for Deaf Tip n°11												
Q23												
Q24												
Average for Deaf Tip n°12												

In the appropriate boxes, write the results of the ten 360° feedback questionnaires. Q1 to Q24 represent the 24 questions, and the numbers 1 to 10, the ten people interviewed.

For each of the 24 questions, add up the scores of boxes 1 to 10, divide the result by 10, and write the number in the corresponding average box.

Then, add up the average of Q1+Q2 to discover your average feedback for Deaf Tip n°1. Proceed respectively with Q3+Q4 for Deaf Tip n°2, Q5+Q6 for Deaf Tip n°3, etc.

Once done, write down for each question the score you gave yourself in the column "Me." Add up the scores of Q1+Q2 to discover the score you gave yourself for Deaf Tip n°1. Do the same with Q3+Q4 for Deaf Tip n°2, Q5+Q6 for Deaf Tip n°3, etc.

Radar chart

To visualize your results, write the twelve totals you have obtained by placing a dot (1 to 10) on the appropriate Deaf Tip axis. Then connect the dots together to create a spider web. Do the same, with a different colored pen, for the twelve totals of your self-assessment.

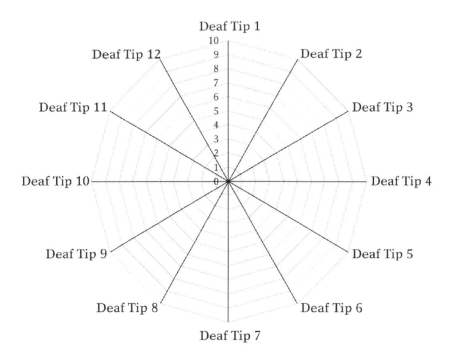

What do you see? Where do the two spider webs overlap? And where do they diverge the most? When you compare your results with the results of your first 360° feedback, what do you see? In which areas did you improve? What could you do to improve even more?

I hope you enjoyed reading *Deaf Tips – Powerful Communication* as much as I did writing it. I am currently working on the next volume of *Deaf Tips* which focuses on effective behaviors specific to the Deaf world. If you would like to share with me your feelings about this first volume or contribute an anecdote to the second volume, please send me an e-mail at contact@deaf-tips.com. I would love to hear from you.

Yours sincerely,

Bruno Paul Kahne

Notes and bibliography

[1] Brown, G. (1999). The Energy of Life. New York, NY: The Free Press.

[2] Hart, L. (1975). How the Brain Works. New York, NY: Basic Books Publishers.

[3] Drubach, D. (2000). The Brain Explained. New Jersey: Prentice-Hall.

[4] Banyai, I. (1995). Zoom. New York, NY: Viking.

[5] The interpretation of Sign Language must be taken cautiously. Despite the proficiency of the interpreter, no one can really render a three dimensional language expressed with unlimited movements of the whole body into a non-dimensional language based on 26 symbols. In the interpretation of Sign Language, the Latin saying *traduttore, traditore* takes on its whole meaning.

[6] Ferguson, R. (Fall 2009). Blind noise and deaf visions: Henry Green's caught, synaesthesia and the blitz. *Journal of Modern Literature*, Volume 33, Issue 1, Pages 102-116.

[7] Deaf people who communicate by means of spoken language.

[8] Place your hand two centimeters away from your lips, and say: *up and down*. Do you feel the difference between the *up* and the *down*? Can you imagine trying to reproduce these puffs of air, their power and direction, without the support of sound?

[9] Weingarten, G. (Sunday, April 8, 2007). Washington Post.

[10] Mehta, R., & Zhu, R. (2009). Blue or red? Exploring the effect of color on cognitive task performances. *Science*, Volume 323, Number 5918, Pages 1226-1229.

[11] Walker, M. (1991). The Power of Color. New York, NY: Avery Publishing Group.

[12] Holland, R. W. (2005). Smells like clean spirit: Nonconscious effects of scent on cognition and behavior. *Psychological Science*, Volume 16, Issue 9, Pages 689-693.

[13] Inspired from Golan, L. (1995). Reading Between the Lips: A Totally Deaf Man Makes It in the Mainstream. Los Angeles, CA: Bonus Books, Page 147.

[14] Sommer, R. (1969). Personal Space. Upper Saddle River, NJ: Prentice-Hall.

[15] Bateson, G., Jackson, D. D., Haley, J. & Weakland, J. (1956) Toward a theory of schizophrenia. *Behavioral Science*, 1, 251-264.

[16] This cultural difference might one day prove Darwin's theory. If Darwin was right, and if Deaf and Hearing people keep on behaving this way, in a few million years, Deaf people will still have legs, while the legs of Hearing

people will have disappeared.

[17] Inspired from Poitras Tucker, B. (1995). The Feel of Silence. Philadelphia, PA: Temple University Press, Page 137.

[18] Hall, E. T. (1966). The Hidden Dimension. Garden City, NY: Doubleday, Pages 121-123.

[19] Hall's intimate (15-45 cm), personal (45-120 cm), social (120-360 cm), and public (360-450 cm or more) distances of course vary according to cultures (how many Italians can you put in an elevator? And how many Americans?).

[20] The sclera is the white part of our eyes which differentiates us from most animals, allowing people to easily detect the slightest movements or changes of the pupil and the iris, informing the observer of the emotions, thoughts, and intentions of others.

[21] Inspired from Uhlberg, M. (2008). Hands of my Father. A Hearing Boy, His Deaf Parents, and the Language of Love, New York, NY: Random House, Pages 112-116.

[22] Inspired from Swiller, J. (2007). The Unheard: A Memoir of Deafness and Africa. New York, NY: Henry Holt & Company, Pages 95, 97, 160, 161.

[23] Inspired from Wright, D. (1969). Deafness: A Personal Account. London, UK: Faber & Faber, Page 109.

[24] Inspired from Golan, L. (1995). Reading Between the Lips: A Totally Deaf Man Makes It in the Mainstream. Los Angeles, CA: Bonus Books, Page 43.

[25] Inspired from Golan, L. (1995). Reading Between the Lips: A Totally Deaf Man Makes It in the Mainstream. Los Angeles, CA: Bonus Books, Page 4.

[26] The only possibility would be to artificially stimulate an emotion in ourselves, and believe at the same time that it is a genuine one. Something that only really good actors and schizophrenic people can do. Even better if they are schizophrenic actors.

[27] According to the ethnological findings of psychologist Paul Ekman (Ekman, 1992:63-69), a Fore tribesman of Papua New Guinea, who has never had any contact with outsiders, can recognize without error emotions such as anger, sadness, fear, surprise, disgust, contempt, and happiness in pictures of people living on other continents.

[28] What was your spouse wearing yesterday? And what color eyes does your manager have?

[29] Inspired from Laborit, E. (1998). The Cry of the Gull. Washington, DC: Gallaudet University Press, Pages 20, 25.

[30] Experiment conducted in May 2011 on a population of 178 men and 88 women, aged 22 to 60 year old from 11 different cultures. The faces were

each time positioned in a different order to avoid any form of preference due to the order of appearance.

[31] Quote from the highly philosophical movie *The House Bunny* (2008), a comedy directed by Fred Wolf.

[32] Bushnell, I. W. (2003). Newborn Face Recognition in the Development of Face Processing in Infancy and Early Childhood. New York, NY: Nova Science Publishers, Page 44.

[33] Kobayashi, N. (1981). Me to me de tashikameru haha to ko no ai. Tokyo: Child Research Net, Retrieved from www.childresearch.net on June 1, 2002.

[34] Simion, F., Macchi Cassia, V., Turati, C., & Valenza, E. (2003). Non-Specific Perceptual Biases at the Origins of Face Processing. In O. Pascalis, & A. Slater, The Development of Face Processing in Infancy and Early Childhood (pp. 13-26). Hauppauge, NY: Nova Science Publishers, Page14.

[35] Gombrich, E. H. (1950). The Story of Art. New York, NY: Phaidon, Page 25.

[36] Inspired from Uhlberg, M. (2008). Hands of my Father. A Hearing Boy, His Deaf Parents, and the Language of Love, New York, NY: Random House, Pages 20-21.

[37] Inspired from Golan, L. (1995). Reading Between the Lips: A Totally Deaf Man Makes It in the Mainstream. Los Angeles, CA: Bonus Books, Page 76.

[38] Huczynski, A. (1993). Management Gurus. London, UK: Routledge, Page 277.

[39] How do you feel when someone talks to you while looking at your nose?

[40] Hall, S. (1983). Train-gone-sorry: the etiquette of social conversations in American Sign Language. *Sign Language Studies*, Volume 41, Pages 291-309.

[41] Delaporte, Y. (2000). Des signes, des noms, des rires. Argentan: ASAS, Page 54.

[42] Peng, F. C. (1974). Kinship signs in Japanese sign language. *Sign Language Studies*, Volume 5, Pages 31-47.

[43] Yau, S. C. (1978). Les signes chinois. Langage gestuel standard des Sourds chinois. Honk-Kong, CN: Editions Langages croisés, Page 209.

[44] For a beautiful example, see Mr. Bean's *Hallelujah*.

[45] Inspired from Poitras Tucker, B. (1995). The Feel of Silence. Philadelphia, PA: Temple University Press, Page 116.

[46] Inspired from Laborit, E. (1998). The Cry of the Gull. Washington, DC: Gallaudet University Press, Page 24.

[47] Inspired from Wright, D. (1969). Deafness: A Personal Account. London, UK: Faber & Faber, Page 112.

[48] My wife's cat's favorite food.

[49] By placing the top of the hand on the bottom lip, then moving it fast

towards the other person.

[50] Inspired from Laborit, E. (1998). The Cry of the Gull. Washington, DC: Gallaudet University Press, Pages 36-37.

[51] A complex form of communication constructed like any language with morphemes around a syntactic system.

[52] Signs conveying in their form the meaning of the object or action represented. The sign for iconicity is made with the right hand grabbing the world and placing it in the palm of the left hand.

[53] A message acted out through exaggerated body motion and/or facial expressions.

[54] Sign Language is different from one country to another, and sometimes there are even different Sign Languages within a single country. In addition, there is no correlation between Sign Language and the spoken language of a country. American Sign Language is for example closer to French Sign Language than to British Sign Language for historical reasons.

[55] Every one of these acronyms can be found in the aviation world.

[56] Goldin-Meadow, S. C. (2008, June 30). The natural order of events: How speakers of different languages represent events nonverbally. *Proceedings of the National Academy of Sciences.*

[57] Hayakawa, S. I. (1939). Language in Thought and Action. Eugene, OR: Harvest Original Publishers.

[58] Inspired from Vasishta, M. (2006). Deaf in Delhi: A Memoir. Washington, DC: Gallaudet University Press, Pages 1-5.

[59] Fustier, M. (2000). Exercices pratiques de communication. Paris, FR: Eyrolles.

[60] Inspired from Oliva, G. (2006-2007). Longing for a group of friends. *Odyssey*, Volume 8, Issue 1, Page 15.

[61] Covey, S. R. (1989). The Seven Habits of Highly Effective People: Restoring the Character Ethic. New York, NY: Free Press, Page 235.

[62] See the description of the zoom exercise in the introduction.

[63] This simple technique forces people to listen carefully instead of preparing their answer when someone is talking.

[64] This statement should not be interpreted to mean that the author supports or even accepts any form of physical abuse.

[65] Köhler, W. (1947). Gestalt Psychology. New York, NY: Liveright, Pages 3-34.

[66] Maurer, D., Pathman, T., & Mondloch, C. J. (2006). The shape of boubas: Sound-shape correspondences in toddlers and adults. *Developmental Science*, Volume 9, Issue 3, Pages 316-322.

[67] Gill, V. (2009, May 28). People may be able to taste words. *BBC News.* http://news.bbc.co.uk/2/hi/science/nature/8070210.stm

[68] Bargh, J. A., Chen, M., & Burrows, L. (1996). Automaticity of social

behavior: Direct effects of trait construct and stereotype activation on action. *Journal of Personality and Social Psychology*, Issue 71, Pages 230-244.

[69] Bargh, J. A., Chen, M., & Burrows, L. (1996). Automaticity of social behavior: Direct effects of trait construct and stereotype activation on action. *Journal of Personality and Social Psychology*, Issue 71, Pages 230-244.

[70] For esthetic reasons, the two original drawings were faithfully reproduced by a professional artist.

[71] Inspired from Golan, L. (1995). Reading Between the Lips: A Totally Deaf Man Makes It in the Mainstream. Los Angeles, CA: Bonus Books, Page 76.

[72] Deaf people use acronyms too. Nobody is perfect.

[73] This is not true for all Deaf people, but the trend is so prevalent that I always ask my Deaf colleagues to arrive one hour before the time I expect them to be there.

[74] See Deaf Tip n°3.

[75] The theory of philosophers such as Plato, Rousseau or Hegel stating that it is language which structures our thoughts is far from being flawless. If language was required to think, how could a baby think himself or herself into language?

[76] It takes about 12 months for a baby to express images in words, and an additional 12 months to move from physically negative forms of expression (facial expression) to oral ones (saying no).

[77] To know if a word belongs to your right brain's inborn language, simply ask yourself if you could paint it. In this paragraph, only the word *brain* can be painted.

[78] Kaup, B. Z. (2007). The experiential view of language comprehension: how is negation represented? F. A. Schmalhofer, in Higher Level Language Processes in the Brain: Inference and Comprehension Processes. Erlbaum, Mahwah, NJ: Routledge, Page 2007.

[79] Virtually, otherwise you won't know what to do next...

[80] This exercise is inspired by Lakoff, 2004.

[81] Especially as there are no penguins at the North Pole.

[82] See Deaf Tip n°5.

[83] See Deaf Tip n°3.

[84] Even if furrowing the eyebrows, shaking the head negatively, and throwing the sign to be negated away from the body are often preferred to specific negative hand signs.

[85] When a double negative is used in Sign Language it is to reinforce the first negation.

[86] American and French Sign Language, for example.

[87] The sign is made with the two index fingers slightly crossed in front of the chest, moving quickly away one from the other like the movement of a

conductor. The sign for different is slightly wider.

[88] Allen, J. (1902). As a Man Thinketh. New York, NY: Thomas Y. Crowell Company Publishers.

[89] This is a reproduction of a drawing attributed to Paul Agule.

[90] Frankl, V. (2006). Man's Search for Meaning. An Introduction to Logotherapy. Boston, MA: Beacon Press.

[91] This technique is also used in the medical world. In some hospitals, to fight illness, instead of focusing on the illness or the pain, patients are taught to visualize white blood cells attacking the disease, turning every infected cell into a healthy one.

[92] I need to sharpen my persuasion skills!

[93] Farb, P. (1974). Word Play: What Happens When People Talk. New York, NY: Alfred A Knopf, Page 222.

[94] Inspired from Vasishta, M. (2006). Deaf in Delhi, A Memoir. Washington, DC: Gallaudet University Press, Pages 216-217.

[95] The end of the *Why* phase.

[96] Inspired from Golan, L. (1995). Reading Between the Lips: A Totally Deaf Man Makes It in the Mainstream. Los Angeles, CA: Bonus Books, Page 258.

[97] Except in places such as aircraft cockpits and operating rooms.

[98] *Err* in Sign Language is expressed by simply showing panic in your eyes!

[99] Deaf people can sometimes be perceived as aggressive by Hearing people. To understand their bluntness please see Deaf Tip n°12.

[100] See Deaf Tip n°2.

[101] Inspired from Galloway, T. (2009). Mean Little Deaf Queer, A Memoir. Boston, MA: Beacon Press, Page 86.

[102] This might be another reason why Hearing society is so uncomfortable with questions. When the powerless start questioning the powerful, trouble is often ahead.

[103] Friedman, T. L. (2003, June 29). Is Google God? *The New York Times*.

[104] Stretching the imagination, one could say that the two names, *Liam* and *Guillaume,* sound slightly the same in French.

[105] Inspired from Golan, L. (1995). Reading Between the Lips: A Totally Deaf Man Makes It in the Mainstream. Los Angeles, CA: Bonus Books, Page 27.

[106] Even if at the time he was already taking drugs to hide his health problems.

[107] This is true in your native tongue as well as for a language you learned later in life.

[108] Rowe, M. L., & Goldin-Meadow , S. (13 February 2009). Differences in early gesture explain SES disparities in child vocabulary size at school entry. *Science*, Volume 323, Issue 5916, Pages 951–953.

[109] See the following chapter.

[110] Inspired from Golan, L. (1995). Reading Between the Lips: A Totally Deaf Man Makes It in the Mainstream. Los Angeles, CA: Bonus Books, Page 62, 331.

[111] Write with your finger, not a pen!

[112] Gerbner, G. (April 1998). Telling stories, or how do we know what we know? The story of cultural indicators and the cultural environment movement. *Wide Angle*, Volume 20, Issue 2, Pages 116-131.

[113] Inspired from Wright, D. (1969). Deafness: A Personal Account. London, UK: Faber & Faber, Page 70.

[114] See Deaf Tip n°8

[115] Remember Deaf Tip n°1

[116] Greene, E. (1996). Storytelling: Art and Technique. Westport, CT: Greenwood Publishing Group, Page 28.

[117] See Deaf Tip n°2

[118] Of course, as seen in the previous chapter, the way a book is written or the way people talk helps.

[119] Pink, D. H. (2005). A Whole New Mind. New York, NY: Riverhead Books, Pages 68-69.

[120] This doesn't mean that when the LH is on, the RH is off. Both hemispheres are always active and complementary. If the LH can recognize a human being from an animal, it needs the RH to recognize who the human being is. If only your LH was active when someone said "I'm dead," you would automatically get ready for the funeral. It is the RH which helps you understand the metaphor.

[121] A native signer is someone born deaf.

[122] Newman, A. J., Bavelier, D., Corina, D., Jezzard, P., & Neville, H. J. (2002). A critical period for right hemisphere recruitment in American Sign Language processing. *Nature Neuroscience*, Volume 5, Pages 76-80.

[123] Sergent, J., Ohta, S., & MacDonald, B. (1992). Functional neuroanatomy of face and object processing. A positron emission tomography study. *Brain*, Volume 115, Pages 15–36.

[124] Davidson, R. J., Shackman, A. J., & Maxwell, J. S. (2004). Asymmetries in face and brain related to emotion. *Trends in Cognitive Sciences*, Volume 8, Pages 389-391.

[125] Tammet, D. (2006). Born on a Blue Day: Inside the Extraordinary Mind of an Autistic Savant. London, UK: Hodder and Stoughton, Pages 11, 21-22, 70, 241.

[126] Uhlberg, L. (2008). Hands of my Father. A Hearing Boy, His Deaf Parents, and the Language of Love, New York, NY: Random House, Pages 29, 111, 112.

[127] University of California - Irvine. Mandarin language is music to the

brain, *Science Daily* (Dec. 12, 2006).

[128] A similar approach was suggested some years ago by Tony Buzan (Buzan, 2003). The Deaf world, however, has been using this technique unconsciously for hundreds of years.

[129] Fellowship of Christian Athletes (2008). Integrity: The Heart and the Soul in Sports. Ventura, CA: Regal, Pages 110-121.

[130] Cormier, S. (2006). La communication et la gestion. Québec: PU Québec, Page 228.

[131] Our brain processes data so quickly that it can incorporate events which have already occurred in our dreams. The clock rings, and in a split second our brain develops a whole scenario to place the ring – which has already occurred – in a logical sequence, the time span between the actual ring and its equivalent in our dream being so short, that the two become one.

[132] See Deaf Tip n°7

[133] e.g., with sane curiosity, and sincere love, not encroaching upon the personal privacy of people, cornering, or jealously checking on them.

[134] Fred was particularly creative in this area!

[135] See Deaf Tip n°2

[136] Unlike when you ask the child to brush his or her teeth, do his or her bed, or empty the dishwasher.

[137] *Money* is *argent* in French.

[138] *Buenos Aires*, is very close to the French *bon air* which means *fresh breeze*.

[139] Montagu, A. (1986). Touching the Human Significance of the Skin. New York, NY: Harper and Row, Page 3.

[140] Prescott, J. W. (1990). Affectional bonding for the prevention of violent behaviors: Neurobiological, psychological and religious/spiritual determinants. In L. J. Hertzberg, G. F. Ostrum, & J. R. Field, Violent behavior Vol. I: Assessment and Intervention (pp. 95-124). Great Neck, NY: PMA Publishing, Pages 95-124.

[141] Field, T. (2002). Violence and touch deprivation in adolescents. *Adolescence*, Volume 37, Pages 735-749.

[142] Field, T. (2001). Massage therapy facilitates weight gain in preterm infants. *Current Directions in Psychological Science*, Volume 10, pages 51-54.

[143] Gueguen, N. V. (2009). The effect of a practitioner's touch on a patient's medication compliance. *Psychology, Health and Medicine,* Volume 14, Issue 6, Pages 689-694.

[144] Eaton, M. M.-B. (1986). The effect of touch on nutritional intake of chronic organic brain syndrome patients. *The Journal of Gerontology*, Volume 41, Issue 5, Pages 611-616.

[145] If you feel that you need to read this sentence over again, don't feel embarrassed, everybody does.

[146] According to Berenson, you can't help but put your hand out to touch

real art (Berenson, 1930).

[147] Think about the last time you went to see a 3D movie. Didn't you try to capture images with your hands?

[148] Montagu, A. (1986). Touching: The Human Significance of the Skin. New York, NY: Harper and Row, Page 124.

[149] Ackerman, J. M. (25 June 2010). Incidental haptic sensations influence social judgments and decisions. *Science*, Volume 328, Issue 5986, Pages 1712-1715.

[150] Williams, L. E., & Bargh, J. A. (24 October 2008). Experiencing physical warmth promotes interpersonal warmth. *Science*, Volume 322, Issue 5901, Pages 606-607.

[151] Inspired from Kisor, H. (1990). What's That Pig Outdoors? A Memoir of Deafness. New York, NY: Hill & Wang, Pages101-102.

[152] Gick, B. D. (26 November 2009). Aero-tactile integration in speech perception. *Nature*, Volume 462, Pages 502-504.

[153] Steward, A. L., & Lupfer, M. (31 Jul 2006). Touching as teaching: the effect of touch on students' perceptions and performance. *Journal of Applied Social Psychology*, Volume 17, Issue 9, Pages 800-809.

[154] Gueguen, N. (2004). Nonverbal encouragement of participation in a course: the effect of touching. *Social Psychology of Education*, Volume 7, Pages 89–98.

[155] Wheldall, K., Bevan, K., & Shortall, K. (1986). A touch of reinforcement: the effects of contingent teacher touch on the classroom behaviour of young children. *Educational Review*, Volume 38, Pages 207–216.

[156] Kraus, M. W., Huang, C., & Keltner, D. (2010). Tactile communication, cooperation, and performance: an ethological study of the NBA. *Emotion*, Volume 10, Issue 5, Pages 745-749.

[157] Hornik, J. (1987). The effect of touch and gaze upon compliance and interest of interviewees. *The Journal of Social Psychology*, Volume 127, Pages 681-683.

[158] Crusco, A. H. (December 1984). The Midas touch: the effects of interpersonal touch on restaurant tipping. *Personality and Social Psychology Bulletin*, Volume 10, Issue 4, Pages 512-517.

[159] Hornik, J. (January 1992). Effects of physical contact on customers' shopping time and behavior. *Marketing Letters*, Volume 3, Issue 1, Pages 49-55.

[160] Guguena, N. (2 June 2007). Courtship compliance: The effect of touch on women's behavior. *Social Influence*, Volume 2, Pages 81-97.

[161] Inspired from Keller, H. (1905). The Story of My Life. New York, NY: Doubleday, Page & Company, Pages 32, 68.

[162] This morning I met a man who had a bag in his right hand and shook my hand with his left. I saw him do the same with all the other people in

the room and thought "That man should read my book!" Then, a few minutes later, sitting next to me, he explained that he was suffering from painful tennis elbow in his right arm and could not shake hands. So, as penance, I decided to learn by heart Deaf Tip n°3, and be less hasty judging people!

[163] Jourard, S. (1972). The Transparent Self: Self-Disclosure and Well-Being. Princeton, NJ: D. Van Norstand Company, Page 192.

[164] Mindess, A. (1999). Reading Between the Signs, Intercultural Communication for Sign Language Interpreters. London, UK: Nicholas Brealey Publishing, Page 102.

[165] In Sign Language, personal pronouns are expressed by pointing at the people they represent. To say *I*, I simply move the index and the ring fingers towards my torso. To say *you*, I move them, pointing them in your direction. Consequently, if someone stands in between my hand and me, *I* becomes *I*, *you*, and *we*.

[166] Inspired from Wright, D. (1969). Deafness: A Personal Account. London, UK: Faber & Faber, Page 81.

[167] Inspired from Wright, D. (1969). Deafness: A Personal Account. London, UK: Faber & Faber, Page 53.

[168] Inspired from Swinbourne, C. (18 June 2008). What's your Sign Name? http://www.bbc.co.uk/ouch/features/sign_names.shtml.

[169] Orwell's Newspeak shows that the fewer words there are in a language, the less people are able to think.

[170] In that case, why do they decide for them what they should be called?

[171] To learn how to ask questions, please see Deaf Tip n°7.

[172] The longer you answer, the more you are in justification.

58209423R00119

Made in the USA
Middletown, DE
05 August 2019